QUICK COOK BOOK

Quick
COOK BOOK
by John Garratt

PELHAM BOOKS

First published in Great Britain by Pelham Books Ltd
52 Bedford Square, London, W.C.1
1973

ISBN 0 7207 0646 7

Set and printed in Great Britain by
Northumberland Press Ltd, Gateshead
in Georgian 11 on 12 point, and bound
by James Burn at Esher, Surrey

To
KENNETH BIRD
who began it all

CONTENTS

FOREWORD

Many of the recipes collected in this book were first published in the magazine *Instant Cookery*, and I should like to thank all those friends and readers, too numerous to name individually, whose ideas and advice formed the basis of some of them.

I am especially indebted to Miss Carol Adler, who has prepared, cooked, and timed each of these recipes and without whose skill and knowledge this book could not have been compiled.

London 1972   John Garratt

INTRODUCTION

More than half of the food we eat in this country today comes from ingredients bought tinned, frozen or dried, and the recipes I have collected in this book recognise this fact. I hope that everyone using the book will find that many attractive and quick-to-prepare dishes can be made using this sort of food.

Often, however, 'fresh' food can be substituted in the recipes if you happen to buy it or have it already in the kitchen. For example, left-over boiled potato can be used in place of canned potato or freshly-made ice-cream instead of the manufactured product.

I have arranged the recipes under seven headings. Within these sections the recipes are arranged under the length of time each takes to prepare, from 5 to 30 minutes.

No recipe need take longer to prepare than the time shown. Some are ready to serve immediately preparation is done. You can quickly identify these because the cooking time given with the preparation time will read NIL, although some will need chilling or time to set.

When an ingredient needs thawing before being used this is printed out in the recipe and time should be allowed for it.

Recipes are for 4 unless otherwise stated, but appetites vary so much that this is only a guide.

Unless otherwise stated, spoon measurements are level.

LIST OF RECIPES

Soups/First Courses

Soups - 5 minutes

CORN CHOWDER

Preparation Time: 5 minutes · Cooking Time: NIL

4 or 5 spring onions
16 oz. can cream-style sweetcorn
10 oz. can cream of mush-
room soup

¾ pint milk
Salt and pepper
Pinch nutmeg

Clean spring onions, removing roots, and slice very thinly including a little of the green part.
Place all ingredients in a saucepan and heat slowly. Do not
allow soup to boil.
Serve very hot.

SHERRIED CHICKEN BROTH

Preparation Time: 5 minutes · Cooking Time: NIL

2 chicken stock cubes
1½ pints boiling water
2 tablespoons dry sherry

Squeeze lemon juice
Salt and pepper

Dissolve the stock cubes in the boiling water.
Stir in sherry and lemon juice, and season to taste.
If desired, serve sprinkled with finely chopped parsley and hand
round Melba toast.

10 minutes

BORTSCH

Preparation Time: 10 minutes · Cooking Time: NIL

12 oz. jar sliced beetroot
15 oz. can consommé
2 tablespoons lemon juice

Salt and pepper
Soured cream

Liquidise the beetroot with 3 tablespoons of its vinegar in an
electric blender, or press the beetroot through a sieve.

Stir remaining vinegar and the lemon juice into the resulting
  purée and season to taste.
Divide among 4 individual soup bowls or glasses.
Drop a little soured cream into each bowl and swirl it round
  with a spoon to make a marble pattern.
Alternatively, the soured cream can be placed in the bases of
  4 stemmed glasses and the soup spooned over it.
Serve chilled.

CORN AND TUNNY FISH CHOWDER

Preparation Time: 10 minutes · Cooking Time: NIL

4⅜ oz. can tunny fish
10½ oz. can condensed cream
  of chicken soup
10 oz. can creamed sweetcorn
½ pint water

1 tablespoon Worcestershire
  sauce
¼ teaspoon salt
Pepper

Drain and flake the tunny fish.
Put in a saucepan with the soup and creamed corn.
Blend in water and Worcestershire sauce.
Bring slowly to simmering point.
Cook 5 minutes, stirring occasionally.
Add seasoning before serving.
Served with crusty French bread and butter. This sustaining
  soup is as good as a meal.

CRAB BISQUE

Preparation Time: 10 minutes · Cooking Time: NIL

6½ oz. can crab
6 oz. can condensed cream of
  tomato soup
1-2 teaspoons lemon juice

¼ pint double cream
½ pint milk
1 tablespoon brandy
Salt and pepper

Drain and flake the crab meat.
Place in a liquidiser with the soup and milk; blend until fairly
  smooth.
Transfer to a saucepan and stir in lemon juice and seasoning.
Heat gently and, when very hot, blend a little of the soup with
  the cream.

Return mixture to the saucepan. Reheat to boiling point, stirring continuously.
Just before serving, stir in the brandy and adjust seasoning.

CRAB AND SWEETCORN SOUP

Preparation Time: 10 minutes · Cooking Time: NIL.

Chicken stock cube
11½ oz. can creamed sweetcorn

1½ oz. can crabmeat
Parsley

Dissolve cube as instructed on packet. Add sweetcorn. Remove spiny bits from crabmeat and add the meat to the dissolved cube and sweetcorn.
Heat through.
Serve sprinkled with parsley

ONION SOUP

Preparation Time: 10 minutes · Cooking Time: NIL

Two 10½ oz. cans condensed onion soup
Salt and freshly ground black pepper

2 slices Emmenthal cheese
4 slices French bread

Dilute soup according to directions on can. Transfer to a saucepan and heat gently.
Season to taste.
Cut the cheese to fit the bread slices and place one piece of cheese on each slice of bread.
Divide hot soup evenly between 4 warmed fireproof soup bowls.
Float one slice of bread, cheese side up, in each bowl and grill.
Cook until cheese bubbles.

YOGHURT AND CUCUMBER SOUP

Preparation Time: 10 minutes · Cooking Time: NIL

1 clove garlic
Salt and pepper
1 small cucumber or ½ large one

Two 5 oz. cartons natural yoghurt (unsweetened)
½ pint milk
1 tablespoon olive oil
1 tablespoon vinegar

Peel garlic, crush with salt.
Cut a few slices from the cucumber and reserve for decoration.
Peel and grate remainder.
Beat yoghurt until smooth, add all other ingredients.
Season.
Serve chilled, garnished with reserved cucumber slices.

15 minutes

BROAD BEAN SOUP

Preparation Time: 15 minutes · Cooking Time: NIL

10 oz. can broad beans
1 bouquet garni
1¼ pints stock made from a
  chicken stock cube
1 rounded teaspoon cornflour
Salt and pepper

Water
¼ pint cream or top of the
  milk
½ oz. butter.
Thin toast

Sieve the broad beans, drained, into a saucepan. Add herbs and
  stock. Bring to the boil.
Blend the cornflour to a smooth paste with water and mix
  quickly into the beans. Season.
Simmer gently for about 5 minutes, adding more stock if the
  soup is too thick.
Remove the bouquet garni and blend in the cream or top of the
  milk.
When ready to serve, stir in the butter.
Serve garnished with tiny squares of thin toast.

CHESTNUT SOUP

Preparation Time: 15 minutes · Cooking Time: 15 minutes

¼ lb. streaky bacon
1 large onion
2 sticks celery
2 chicken stock cubes

15½ oz. can unsweetened chestnut purée
1½ pints boiling water
½ pint milk
Salt and pepper

Remove rinds from bacon, fry until crisp. Drain on absorbent paper then chop finely.

Peel and chop the onion. Chop the celery finely. Fry these vegetables in the bacon fat until transparent, adding more fat if necessary.

Dissolve stock cubes in boiling water. Gradually blend into the chestnut purée. Add to pan, and simmer, covered, for 15 minutes.

Add the milk, reheat gently and season.

Serve the soup with the chopped bacon.

CHILLED AVOCADO AND PRAWN SOUP

Preparation Time: 15 minutes · Cooking Time: NIL

2 large ripe avocado pears
½ pint chicken stock
1 tablespoon wine vinegar
¼ teaspoon instant orange peel or grated rind ½ orange
2 spring onions or 1 teaspoon dried chives
½ teaspoon dried mint or 1 sprig fresh mint
½ pint cultured buttermilk
Salt and pepper
¼ pint milk
4 oz. peeled prawns

Scoop flesh from avocados. Blend until smooth in a liquidiser with stock, vinegar, orange peel, sliced spring onions or chives and the mint. Add buttermilk, fresh milk and seasoning. Alternatively, sieve the avocado flesh, add finely chopped onions and mint and stir in remaining ingredients, except the prawns. Chill.

Garnish with prawns.

CHINESE CHICKEN SOUP

Preparation Time: 15 minutes · Cooking Time: NIL

2 chicken stock cubes
2 pints boiling water
1 stick celery
1 dessertspoon instant onion
2 oz. button mushrooms
1 oz. Chinese noodles

Dissolve stock cubes in the water.

Wash and slice the celery and add to stock with the onion. Bring to boil and simmer for 2-3 minutes

Slice the mushrooms.

When the soup boils, add noodles and mushrooms and cook until noodles are tender; about 5 minutes.

CREAM OF CARROT AND CELERY SOUP

Preparation Time: 15 minutes · Cooking Time: NIL

10 oz. can carrots
14 oz. can celery hearts
¾ pint chicken stock
1 dessertspoon instant onion
½ pint milk

½ oz. butter
2 tablespoons single cream
Salt and pepper
Chopped parsley
Fried croûtons

Drain carrots and celery. Add the onion to the hot stock.

Purée the vegetables with the stock. Place purée in a saucepan with the milk and butter, add seasoning to taste and heat gently to boiling point.

Stir in cream off the heat. Transfer to a tureen or individual soup bowls, and serve sprinkled with chopped parsley. Serve croûtons separately.

CREAM OF SPINACH SOUP

Preparation Time: 15 minutes · Cooking Time: NIL

12 oz. carton frozen chopped spinach
¾ oz. butter or margarine
¾ oz. flour

¼ teaspoon grated nutmeg
1 pint milk
Salt and pepper

Cook spinach according to directions on packet.

Purée spinach and its liquid in an electric blender.

Place butter (or margarine), flour and milk in a saucepan with the seasonings and whisk over a moderate heat until smoothly blended. Bring to the boil, stirring, and simmer for 2-3 minutes.

Stir in spinach purée and adjust seasoning.

Reheat before serving.

GAZPACHO

Preparation Time: 15 minutes · Cooking Time: NIL

2 tablespoons olive oil	½ medium-sized cucumber
14 oz. can tomato juice	8½ oz. can roasted pimentos
Few drops chili sauce	1 small onion
Black pepper	1 clove garlic
1 teaspoon salt	1½ tablespoons wine vinegar.

Whisk oil gradually into tomato juice. Add chili sauce, pepper and salt and mix well.

Skin the cucumber and dice finely; drain the pimentos and chop them.

Add the cucumber, pimentos, grated onion, crushed garlic and vinegar to tomato mixture.

Chill thoroughly before serving.

LEMON CHICKEN SOUP

Preparation Time: 15 minutes · Cooking Time: NIL

Two 15 oz. cans clear chicken broth	1 lemon
	Salt and pepper
3 eggs	Chopped chives

Slightly warm the chicken broth in a saucepan.

Beat the eggs together with the grated lemon rind and lemon juice.

Add some of the warmed soup and mix well; then blend with remaining soup.

Heat very gently until soup thickens, but do not boil, stirring constantly.

Allow to cool and then refrigerate until very cold; season with salt and pepper.

Serve with chopped chives.

ORANGE AND TOMATO SOUP

Preparation Time: 15 minutes · Cooking Time: NIL

1 lb. ripe tomatoes or ½ pint canned tomato juice
½ pint fresh orange juice, strained
Juice of ½ lemon

Salt and pepper
Celery salt
Orange rind or mint sprigs to garnish

Peel the tomatoes, slice and sieve; or liquidise in an electric blender.
Alternatively, use ½ pint canned tomato juice.
Combine with fruit juice.
Season with salt, pepper and celery salt.
Serve chilled, garnished with strips of blanched orange rind or with mint sprigs.

POTATO SOUP

Preparation Time: 15 minutes · Cooking Time: NIL

1 large onion
1½ pints water
1 chicken stock cube
4 oz. packet frozen mixed vegetables

5-6 serving packet instant mashed potato
¼ pint milk
Salt and pepper
½ oz. butter

Peel the onion and chop finely. Place in a pan with the water, stock cube and mixed vegetables. Bring to the boil and allow to simmer for 8 minutes until the vegetables are cooked.
Remove from heat and stir in the potato. Add the milk. Season.
Reheat to boiling point. Stir in the butter.
Serve with croûtons.
This soup thickens on standing, so, if prepared in advance, it will be necessary to add more stock before serving.

QUICK COUNTRY CHOWDER

Preparation Time: 15 minutes · Cooking Time: NIL

3-4 serving packet chicken and leek soup
1 pint water

10 oz. can new potatoes
3 oz. cheese
Chopped chives

Make up the soup as directed.

Drain the potatoes and cut into dice. Add to soup and heat gently for 5 minutes.

Cut the cheese into small dice and stir into soup.

Serve sprinkled with chopped chives.

Serves 3.

20 minutes

BANANA SOUP

Preparation Time: 20 minutes · Cooking Time: NIL

4 ripe bananas
Juice ½ lemon
1-2 oz. sugar
½ pint milk

Grated rind of an orange
1 dessertspoon cornflour
Maraschino cherries

Peel and mash the bananas.

Purée in an electric blender or through a sieve, adding the lemon juice during this process to prevent discoloration.

Add milk, sugar and salt and grated orange rind. In a saucepan, bring the mixture to the boil.

Mix the cornflour with a little cold water, add to the saucepan and stir over heat until mixture thickens slightly.

Allow to cool, then refrigerate.

Serve well-chilled, garnishing each portion with a drained maraschino cherry.

CHICKEN BROCCOLI SOUP

Preparation Time: 20 minutes · Cooking Time: NIL

9 oz. packet broccoli spears
Chicken stock cube
½ pint milk
¼ pint double cream

10½ oz. can condensed cream of chicken soup
Salt and pepper

Cook the broccoli spears according to the instructions on the packet, but use the stock cube instead of salting the water.

Drain well, reserving ½ pint of the liquid. Combine broccoli, reserved liquid, milk, cream and undiluted soup.

Blend in a liquidiser for about 30 seconds, or until smooth.
Return to the rinsed-out pan and heat through, but do not boil.
Season to taste.
Serves 6.

MINTED PEA SOUP

Preparation Time: 20 minutes · Cooking Time: NIL

8 oz. frozen garden peas, mint
  flavoured
½ oz. butter
1 tablespoon flour

½ pint milk
2 tablespoons single cream
Salt and pepper

Cook the peas in 8 fluid ounces lightly-salted water until rather
  softer than normal. Pass the entire contents through a sieve
  to form a purée (or use a liquidiser).
Melt the butter in a saucepan, stir in the flour off the heat. Cook
  over a low heat, stirring constantly, for 2 minutes.
Remove from heat and gradually blend in the milk.
Return and bring to the boil, stirring constantly.
Simmer for 3 minutes. Stir in the pea purée.
Allow to cool slightly, then add the cream. Season.
Serve hot or cold.

25 minutes

CHILLED CUCUMBER SOUP

Preparation Time: 25 minutes · Cooking Time: NIL

1 oz. butter
1 cucumber, peeled and
  chopped
1 onion, chopped
¾ pint water

1½ pint packet chicken noodle
  soup
¼ pint single cream
¼ pint milk

Melt butter and sauté the cucumber and onion until onion is
  soft (about 5 minutes).
Add the water, bring to the boil, then stir in the contents of the
  packet of soup and simmer for 7 minutes.

Blend in a liquidiser, then stir in cream and milk.
Chill.
Serve garnished with slices of cucumber.
Serves 4-6.

30 minutes

LETTUCE SOUP

Preparation Time: 30 minutes · Cooking Time: NIL

2 lettuces	½ pint chicken stock
4 spring onions	¼ pint single cream
2 oz. butter	Salt and pepper
½ pint milk	Sugar

Wash and shred the lettuces.
Slice the spring onions.
Melt the butter in a saucepan, add the vegetables and cook over
   a very gentle heat for 10 minutes.
Add the milk and stock.
Cover and simmer for 15 minutes, then pass through a sieve
   or use a blender.
Return soup to rinsed-out saucepan. Stir in the cream and season
   to taste with salt, pepper and sugar.
Reheat but do not boil.
Serve chilled.

RHUBARB SOUP

Preparation Time: 30 minutes · Cooking Time: NIL

2 lb. rhubarb	1 tablespoon cornflour
2 pints water	¼ pint double cream
4-6 oz. sugar	1 egg yolk

Wash the rhubarb; remove leaves and cut stems into 1 inch
   pieces.
Put in a saucepan with the water. Cook over a gentle heat until
   rhubarb is mushy. Rub through a sieve or liquefy in an electric blender.

Stir in the sugar.

Return to rinsed-out saucepan.

Mix cornflour with a little water.

Add it to hot soup, bring to boil and stir over heat until soup has thickened slightly.

Combine cream and beaten egg yolk.

Stir a little hot soup into this mixture then return to contents of pan.

Stir over gentle heat for a few minutes, but do not allow soup to boil.

Chill.

Serve with sweet biscuits.

First Courses - 5 minutes

CREAM CHEESE STARTER

Preparation Time: 5 minutes · Cooking Time: NIL

3 oz. packet semi-salted cream
   cheese

4½ oz. packet processed cream
   cheese
10½ oz. can consommé

Combine the two cheeses and mix together until smooth.
Gradually blend in the consommé.
Spoon into individual dishes and refrigerate until set.
Serve with Melba toast.

10 minutes

ANCHOVY WITH APPLE

Preparation Time: 10 minutes · Cooking Time: NIL

2 eating apples
2 oz. can anchovies
¼ pint mayonnaise

1 small lettuce
Lemon slices

Peel the apples and remove cores.
Cut flesh into dice.
Drain the anchovies and cut into small pieces.
Blend apples and anchovies with the mayonnaise until well-
   coated.
Chill.
Wash and shred the lettuce and arrange on 4 small plates.
Divide the apple and anchovy mixture between the plates and
   serve garnished with lemon slices.

CRAB AVOCADO STARTER

Preparation Time: 10 minutes · Cooking Time: NIL

2 avocado pears
4 oz. can crab meat

Mayonnaise

Slice pears lengthwise and remove the stones. Carefully remove the flesh and dice it. Combine with mayonnaise and drained, flaked crabmeat. Divide mixture between the 4 halves.

EGG MOUSSE
Preparation Time: 10 minutes · Cooking Time: NIL

4 hardboiled eggs
10½ oz. can consommé
4 fl. oz. cream

1 dessertspoon Worcestershire sauce
Salt and pepper

Shell the eggs and chop roughly. Put them in an electric blender with consommé, cream and sauce.
Blend for about 30 seconds or until smooth. Season.
Pour into ramekins or one large bowl.
Refrigerate until set.

PEACHES WITH CREAM CHEESE
Preparation Time: 10 minutes · Cooking Time: NIL

6 canned peach halves
2 oz. butter
Two 3 oz. packets cream cheese

Salt and pepper
Paprika
Watercress

Drain the peach halves from their syrup.
Cream together butter and cheese.
Season to taste.
Spoon or pipe mixture into hollows of peach halves.
Place on individual plates and serve chilled, sprinkled with paprika and garnished with watercress.
This recipe can also be made with fresh peaches or nectarines.

POTTED TUNA
Preparation Time: 10 minutes · Cooking Time: NIL

7 oz. can tuna
2 oz. butter
Freshly ground black pepper

A little grated nutmeg
Salt

Drain any liquid from tin of tuna.

Melt butter in a basin over a pan of hot water.

Remove bowl from water, add flaked tuna and pound with butter.

Season to taste with freshly ground black pepper and a little grated nutmeg, adding a little salt if necessary.

Turn into a small dish or pot and cover with a piece of buttered paper.

Refrigerate.

Unmould onto lettuce leaves, and serve with brown bread and butter.

This recipe can also be made with tinned salmon.

PRAWN AND GRAPE COCKTAIL

Preparation Time: 10 minutes · Cooking Time: NIL

1 tablespoon fruity sauce	Watercress
5 fl. oz. carton soured cream	4 oz. cooked prawns
4 oz. green grapes	Lemon wedges

Blend together the fruity sauce and soured cream. Chill. Wash the grapes, cut them in half, and remove pips.

To serve: roughly chop the watercress and divide among 4 individual dishes. Mix together prepared sauce, halved grapes and thawed prawns.

Spoon onto watercress and serve with lemon wedges.

SPICED GRAPEFRUIT

Preparation Time: 10 minutes · Cooking Time: NIL

2 large grapefruit	2 tablespoons sherry
2 oz. soft brown sugar	1 oz. butter
½ teaspoon mixed spice	Glacé or maraschino cherries

Halve grapefruit. Using a sharp, serrated knife, cut into segments and discard pips and pith.

Sprinkle with brown sugar, mixed spice and sherry.

Dot with small knobs of butter.

Cook under a grill on medium heat for 4-5 minutes, or in a moderately hot oven, gas mark 6, 400° F., for 8-10 minutes.

Serve hot with a cherry on each.

STUFFED PEAR STARTER

Preparation Time: 10 minutes · Cooking Time: NIL

15 oz. can pear halves
1 bunch watercress or 1 box cress

10 oz. preserved ginger
4 oz. cottage cheese

Drain pears.
Wash and dry cress.
Arrange on 6 small plates. Put a pear half on each, cut side uppermost.
Chop ginger very finely.
Mix well with cottage cheese.
Spoon into pear cavities. Sprinkle with paprika.
Chill at least 30 minutes before serving.

STUFFED VINE LEAVES—EGG AND LEMON SAUCE

Preparation Time: 10 minutes · Cooking Time: NIL

8 oz. can stuffed vine leaves (dolmades)
1 egg yolk

2½ fl. oz. chicken or vegetable stock
Juice ½ lemon

Arrange the vine leaves on 4 small plates.
Place the egg yolk in a basin and whisk in the stock and lemon juice.
Place bowl in a pan containing hot water over a gentle heat and whisk egg mixture until thick and frothy: about 5-7 minutes.
Do not allow water to boil or mixture to become too hot.
Spoon sauce over vine leaves and serve immediately.

15 minutes

BRUGES EGG SAVOURY

Preparation Time: 15 minutes · Cooking Time: 10-15 minutes

3 eggs
1 teaspoon chopped chives
1 teaspoon chopped parsley
½ teaspoon French mustard
2 oz. peeled prawns

6 oz. can cream
2 oz. processed Gruyère cheese
Extra chopped parsley
Salt and pepper

Butter 3 individual fireproof dishes.
Hard-boil eggs and slice.
Mix together the sliced eggs, chopped chives, mustard, prawns and cream, and season to taste.
Divide the mixture evenly between the 3 fireproof dishes.
Sieve the cheese and sprinkle over each dish.
Bake at gas mark 6, 400° F., for 10-15 minutes.
Serve sprinkled with extra chopped parsley.

CHEESE AND ASPARAGUS SOUFFLÉ

Preparation Time: 15 minutes · Cooking Time: 10-15 minutes

10½ oz. can cut asparagus
spears
About 6 fl. oz. milk

½ pint packet cheese sauce
mix
3 eggs
Salt and pepper

Drain asparagus, reserving the liquid. Purée the asparagus in a blender, or push through a sieve.
Put the liquid from the can into a measuring jug and make it up to ½ pint with milk.
Make up the cheese sauce following directions on the packet, using the milk and asparagus liquid mixture.
Separate the eggs. Allow the sauce to cool slightly, then pour onto the beaten yolks. Stir in the asparagus purée. Season.
Beat the egg whites stiffly and fold gently into the mixture.
Transfer to a buttered soufflé or ovenproof dish.

Cook in a moderate oven, gas mark 5, 375° F., until well risen and lightly set throughout.
Serve immediately.

CHEESE PÂTÉ

Preparation Time: 15 minutes · Cooking Time: NIL

1 oz. butter
1 oz. flour
¼ pint milk
4 oz. grated Cheddar cheese
1 tablespoon mayonnaise.
4 stuffed olives

1 clove garlic
Salt and pepper
Good pinch cayenne pepper
Pinch dry mustard
Hot toast

Melt the butter in a small saucepan, stir in the flour and cook the mixture for 2-3 minutes. Remove from heat and gradually blend in the milk.

Return to heat and stir until mixture boils and thickens. Continue cooking for 2 minutes.

Remove from heat and stir in cheese. Then add the mayonnaise, chopped olives, the garlic (crushed with a little salt) and seasonings to taste.

Turn mixture into a small dish or 4 individual dishes, cover and keep in a refrigerator or cool place until needed.

Serve chilled with hot toast.

COD'S ROE PÂTÉ

Preparation Time: 15 minutes · Cooking Time: NIL

7 oz. can cod roe
6 tablespoons vegetable oil
1½ tablespoons vinegar
Pepper

2 teaspoons grated onion
2 tablespoons fresh chopped parsley

Beat cod's roe with 2 tablespoons oil until smooth.

Then beat in, alternately, vinegar and enough oil to produce a creamy pâté.

Add them gradually, you may need only 2 tablespoons of oil.

Season with pepper, onion and parsley.

Chill.

CORN AND PRAWN RAMEKINS
Preparation Time: 15 minutes · Cooking Time: NIL

4 oz. Gouda cheese	4 oz. shelled prawns
4 hardboiled eggs	1 tablespoon chopped parsley
10 oz. can cream-style corn	Salt and pepper

Grate the cheese. Shell and chop the hardboiled eggs.
Place the corn, hardboiled eggs, prawns and chopped parsley in a saucepan with half the grated cheese. Season well.
Heat gently, stirring from time to time, until very hot.
Spoon into 4 individual dishes and top with the remaining grated cheese.
Brown under a hot grill and serve immediately with hot buttered toast.

CRAB MOUSSE
Preparation Time: 15 minutes · Cooking Time: NIL

½ oz. gelatine	1 dessertspoon brandy
Two 3½ oz. cans crab	Salt and pepper
Juice of 1 lemon	4 oz. can cream
3 tablespoons mayonnaise	1 egg white

Soften gelatine in a little cold water. Drain and flake crab-meat, reserving a few larger pieces for decoration.
Heat lemon juice, pour onto softened gelatine and stir until dissolved.
Stir mayonnaise and brandy into crab-meat.
Shake cream in can, stir until smooth, fold into shellfish mixture and add seasoning to taste.
Stir in lemon juice and gelatine.
Beat egg white until stiff and fold in lightly. Transfer to a serving-dish. Decorate top with reserved pieces of crab-meat.
Refrigerate until set.

CREAMY PÂTÉ

Preparation Time: 15 minutes · Cooking Time: NIL

6 oz. liver sausage
3 oz. packet cream cheese
⅛ teaspoon instant garlic
  powder
2 tablespoons dry cherry

Salt and pepper
Slices of gherkin
Strips canned pimentos
10½ fl. oz. can condensed consommé

Thoroughly blend together the liver sausage and softened cream
  cheese. Add the garlic powder, 1 tablespoon sherry and salt
  and pepper to taste.
Divide mixture equally between 4 individual ramekin—or
  similar—dishes. Smooth over top.
Decorate each one with slices of gherkin and strips of drained
  pimentos.
Stir remaining sherry into consommé. Spoon it over the pâté
  to cover decoration. Chill until set.
Serve with brown bread and butter.

CORN AND CUCUMBER SALAD

Preparation Time: 15 minutes · Cooking Time: NIL

6 oz. packet frozen sweetcorn
Salt and pepper
Pinch dry mustard
2 tablespoons olive oil
1 tablespoon vinegar

2 hardboiled eggs, shelled
6-inch piece of cucumber,
  peeled
Lettuce leaves

Cook the sweetcorn according to the directions. Drain and cool.
Prepare the dressing by placing the seasonings in a basin, add
  the oil and then gradually add the vinegar, mixing well.
Chop eggs. Dice cucumber.
Toss the hardboiled eggs, cucumber and sweetcorn in the
  dressing.
Serve chilled on the lettuce in individual glasses.

EGGS IN MAYONNAISE WITH PAPRIKA

Preparation Time: 15 minutes · Cooking Time: NIL

8 tablespoons mayonnaise
1 dessertspoon Worcestershire sauce
1 dessertspoon tomato purée
1 teaspoon lemon juice

½ teaspoon paprika
Pinch curry powder
1 bunch watercress
4 hardboiled eggs
Extra pakrika

Blend mayonnaise with the next five ingredients.
Shell eggs and halve lengthwise.
Arrange washed watercress sprigs on 4 small plates. Add eggs, cut side down. Spoon the sauce over them and garnish with a dash of paprika on each egg.

EGG PEPPERS

Preparation Time: 15 minutes · Cooking Time: 20 minutes

2 large green peppers
1½ oz. fresh breadcrumbs
1 oz. melted butter

1 teaspoon dried parsley
Salt and pepper
4 eggs

Halve the peppers lengthwise, remove ribs and seeds and blanch in boiling water for 10 minutes.
Drain and refresh under cold water. Place, hollow sides up, in a buttered overproof dish.
Meanwhile, combine the breadcrumbs, melted butter, parsley and salt and pepper. Divide between the peppers and place in the base of each one.
Break an egg onto the breadcrumb mixture in each paper.
Bake in a moderate oven, gas mark 4, 350° F., for 20 minutes or until eggs are cooked to taste.

FRIED SPINACH

Preparation Time: 15 minutes · Cooking Time: NIL

11 oz. packet frozen chopped spinach
1 egg
Salt and pepper

2 tablespoons grated cheese
3 oz. white breadcrumbs
Oil for frying

Cook the spinach according to the directions on the packet.

Drain, and press out all the water. Chop well.

Mix in the egg, salt and pepper, and the grated cheese.

Divide into 6 pieces.

Roll them in the white breadcrumbs and fry quickly in the oil until brown.

PRAWNS IN CURRY SOURED CREAM SAUCE

Preparation Time: 15 minutes · Cooking Time: NIL

1 small onion	5 oz. carton soured cream
1 oz. butter	Salt and pepper
1 teaspoon curry powder	½ cucumber
6½ oz. can peeled prawns	Paprika

Peel and chop the onion. Melt butter in a saucepan and soften onion in it.

Add curry powder and cook 1-2 minutes, stirring all the time.

Add drained and rinsed prawns and sauté 1-2 minutes.

Allow to cool, then stir in soured cream and season to taste.

Serve chilled on a bed of finely sliced cucumber in individual dishes.

Sprinkle with paprika pepper.

PRAWN PUFFS

Preparation Time: 15 minutes · Cooking Time: NIL

13 oz. packet frozen thawed haddock fillets	Salt and pepper
4 oz. packet frozen, thawed peeled prawns	1 tablespoon anchovy essence or tomato purée
Juice of 1 lemon	5 oz. self-raising flour
	Fat or oil for deep frying

Remove skin from the thawed haddock. Chop flesh.

Chop thawed prawns and mix with the fish.

Add lemon juice, salt and pepper, and anchovy essence or tomato purée. Sift in the flour and mix in thoroughly.

Divide the mixture into 32 portions and roll into small balls, using floured hands.

Fry in hot fat or oil for 4-5 minutes or until golden-brown and cooked through. Drain on absorbent paper.

Serve hot on cocktail sticks with mayonnaise and tomato dip.

RATATOUILLE

Preparation Time: 15 minutes · Cooking Time: NIL

2 onions	14¾ oz. can aubergines in oil
2 tablespoons olive oil	8 oz. can tomatoes
1 green pepper	1 clove garlic
2-3 courgettes	Salt and pepper

Peel and slice the onions. Sauté in the oil until transparent.

Halve the pepper and remove the pith and seeds. Cut into thin strips. Add to the pan and continue cooking gently.

Wash the courgettes and remove stalks. Cut into slices, ¼ inch in width, slantwise. Add to pan.

Stir in the aubergines, tomatoes, garlic crushed with a little salt, and salt and pepper to taste.

Cover and simmer for about 5-10 minutes or until courgettes are just tender.

SEAFOOD STARTER

Preparation Time: 15 minutes · Cooking Time: 15 minutes

13 oz. packet frozen smoked haddock	2½ fl. oz. fresh cream
	Parmesan cheese
8 oz. can tomatoes	

Cook haddock as directed on packet. Meanwhile, butter individual fireproof ramekin dishes.

Flake the cooked fish and mix with the cream and tomatoes. The mixture should be sauce-like, not stiff.

Sprinkle grated cheese on top and bake in a fairly hot oven for 15 minutes.

20 minutes

SPINACH TIMBALES
Preparation Time: 20 minutes · Cooking Time: 30 minutes

12 oz. packet frozen chopped
  spinach
½ pint packet onion sauce mix
½ pint milk
3 egg yolks

Salt and pepper
¼ teaspoon grated nutmeg
½ pint packet hollandaise
  sauce mix
1 tablespoon salad oil

Cook the spinach according to directions on packet; drain.

Make up the onion sauce mix, using the milk, and following packet instructions.

Pour a little of the sauce onto the beaten egg yolks, stirring all the time. Return to saucepan off the heat and mix in. Add the spinach. Season with salt, pepper and nutmeg.

Divide this mixture between 8 buttered castle pudding or dariole moulds. Stand them in a roasting tin containing hot water and cook in a moderate oven, gas mark 4, 350° F., until set (about 30 minutes). Unmould.

While the moulds are cooking, make up the hollandaise sauce using oil and water according to packet instructions.

Spoon the sauce over the cooked spinach timbales or round their bases.

Serve hot.

STUFFED EGGS WITH PRAWNS
Preparation Time: 20 minutes · Cooking Time: NIL

4 eggs
4 anchovies
2¾ oz. (drained weight) can of
  prawns

2 oz. butter
4 tablespoons tomato ketchup
Salt and cayenne pepper

Hard-boil the eggs, shell and cut in half lengthways.

Put the yolks into a bowl.

Add the chopped anchovies, butter and seasoning and mash together thoroughly.

Spoon or pipe the mixture back into the egg whites.

Put them on a heatproof dish with the rest of the filling in the centre of the dish.

Grill lightly until warmed through.

Spoon hot tomato ketchup round the eggs and garnish with the drained and rinsed prawns.

STUFFED TOMATOES

Preparation Time: 20 minutes · Cooking Time: NIL

1 tablespoon dried mixed peppers	4 tablespoons cooked rice
	Salt and pepper
2 rashers bacon	Pinch of basil
4 large tomatoes	Watercress

Soak the peppers in boiling water for 5 minutes. Strain.

Remove rinds from bacon and fry until crisp. Cut into small pieces.

Cut tops off tomatoes and scoop out centres. Put aside.

Mix together the rice, peppers and bacon.

Add the tomato centres.

Season with salt, pepper and a pinch of basil.

Fill mixture into tomato cases and top with lids.

Serve on a bed of watercress.

CHAMPIGNONS À LA GRÈCQUE

Preparation Time: 25 minutes · Cooking Time: NIL

¼ lb. tiny onions	1 bayleaf
3 tablespoons olive oil	Salt and pepper
¼ pint dry white wine	½ lb. button mushrooms
2½ fl. oz. chicken stock	2-3 tomatoes
Juice 1 lemon	

Peel the onions and place in a saucepan with the olive oil, wine, stock, lemon juice, bayleaf and seasoning.

Simmer for 10 minutes, then add the quartered mushrooms and the peeled and quartered tomatoes.

Continue to simmer for a further 5-10 minutes.

Adjust seasoning. Transfer to a serving dish.

Snacks

Snacks - 5 minutes

CHEESY POTATOES

Preparation Time: 5 minutes · Cooking Time: 10 minutes

3-4 serving packet instant
  mashed potato
1 egg, beaten

4-6 oz. cheese
French mustard

Make up the potato as directed, and beat in the egg, leaving a
  little for brushing over the potato before baking.
Cut cheese in pieces 1 inch square and 3/4 inch thick, and spread
  with a little French mustard.
Place cheese pieces in a dish and fork potato mixture on top.
Brush potato with a little left-over beaten egg and bake in
  moderate oven, gas mark 4 or 350° F., for 10 minutes until
  pale golden brown.
Good served with sausages.

CINNAMON AND CLOVE TOFFEE TOAST

Preparation Time: 5 minutes · Cooking Time: NIL

8 slices bread
1 oz. butter
½ teaspoon ground cinnamon

Pinch ground cloves
4 oz. golden syrup

Toast the bread on both sides.
Meanwhile, blend together the remaining ingredients.
Spread on the toast and grill until bubbly.

SAVOURY MERINGUE TOAST

Preparation Time: 5 minutes · Cooking Time: 10 minutes

1 egg, separated
Round of buttered toast

¼ oz. grated Parmesan cheese
Salt and pepper

Put yolk on round of toast.
Whisk white stiffly, season and fold in the cheese.
Pile on toast and grill gently for about 10 minutes until firm
  and golden brown. Serves one.

10 minutes

BAKED ASPARAGUS ROLLS

Preparation Time: 10 minutes · Cooking Time: 12-15 minutes

10-12 thin slices bread
10½ oz. can asparagus

4 oz. grated Cheddar cheese
Melted butter

Remove crusts from bread and trim, if necessary, so that width of slice is the same as the length of the asparagus spears.
Flatten bread slices with a rolling pin.
Sprinkle each slice with grated cheese and place 3 drained asparagus spears across each piece of bread.
Form the slices into rolls and secure with cocktail sticks.
Brush with melted butter.
Bake in a hot oven, gas mark 7, 425° F., for 12-15 minutes until bread is crisp and golden.
Serve hot.
Makes 10-12 rolls.

BEEF AND HORSERADISH FRIED SANDWICH

Preparation Time: 10 minutes · Cooking Time: NIL

1 teaspoon horseradish sauce
1¼ oz. jar beef spread
1 tomato

2 slices bread from a large loaf
Fat or oil for frying

Mix the sauce with the spread.
Slice the tomato.
Spread one side of each slice of bread with half the beef mixture.
Sandwich the slices together with the tomato in between.
Cut in four.
Fry in a little hot fat or oil until golden and crisp on both sides.
Serve at once.
Serves one.

CHEESE IN PASTRY

Preparation Time: 10 minutes · Cooking Time: 20-25 minutes

7½ oz. packet frozen short-   ¼ lb. Danish blue cheese.
  crust pastry

Roll the thawed pastry into a square the thickness of a penny.
Spread the cheese on one half of the square.
Fold the other half over and seal it.
Pierce 3 small holes in the top and bake in a hot oven, gas mark
  7, 425° F., for 20-25 minutes.

CORNED BEEF ROLLS

Preparation Time: 10 minutes · Cooking Time: 10-15 minutes

6 round bread rolls   Onion salt
7 oz. can corned beef   Worcestershire sauce
4 oz. cheese

Take tops off bread rolls and remove soft insides.
Chop corned beef and grate the cheese.
Mix beef and cheese with onion salt and sauce. Fill rolls with
  this filling and replace tops.
Bake at gas mark 6, 400° F., for 10-15 minutes until heated
  through.

CROQUE MONSIEUR

Preparation Time: 10 minutes · Cooking Time: NIL

8 thin slices bread   2 eggs
Butter   Little milk
4 thin slices ham   Pinch salt
4 thin slices mild Derby,   3 oz. butter
  Double Gloucester or Ched-   4 tablespoons vegetable oil
  dar cheese

Spread the bread slices with butter.
Place a slice of ham and a slice of cheese on four of the pieces of
  bread, and top each with remaining bread slices.
Press sandwiches gently together and cut off crusts.

Beat the eggs with a little milk and add a pinch of salt.

Heat the butter and oil in a wide shallow pan.

When really hot, dip the sandwiches in the egg and milk mixture and quickly fry them to a golden brown on both sides.

Serve immediately.

CROQUE HOLLANDAISE

Preparation Time: 10 minutes · Cooking Time: NIL

12 oz. can pork luncheon meat
12 slices buttered bread

12 slices processed cheese
Butter or oil for frying

Cut the luncheon meat into 6 slices.

Make 6 sandwiches, each containing 2 slices processed cheese with a slice of luncheon meat in between.

Trim the crusts from the sandwiches and cut each one in half.

Fry in hot oil or butter until bread is crisp on the outside and the cheese has melted inside.

Serve hot.

CROSTINI NAPOLITAN

Preparation Time: 10 minutes · Cooking Time: 12-15 minutes

4 thick slices bread
4 slices processed cheese
1¾ oz. can anchovy fillets
2 tomatoes

Oregano
Black pepper
A little oil

Remove the crusts from the bread, cut the bread into triangles and lay on a well-oiled oven tray.

Cut the cheese into triangles and place on bread.

Rinse the anchovy fillets in warm water and lattice them across the cheese.

Skin and slice the tomatoes. Lay slices on top of cheese.

Sprinkle with oregano and black pepper and a few drops of oil.

Bake for 12-15 minutes at gas mark 3, 325° F., until the bread is crisp and the cheese is melting.

DEVILLED STRAWS

Preparation Time: 10 minutes · Cooking Time: 15 minutes

7½ oz. packet frozen puff
pastry
1 oz. butter
1 teaspoon curry powder

½ teaspoon Worcestershire
sauce
1 oz. potato crisps

Roll out the pastry on a lightly-floured board to a rectangle
about 12 inches by 10 inches.

Melt the butter. Remove from heat and stir in the curry powder
and Worcestershire sauce.

Brush this mixture over the pastry, then sprinkle with crushed
potato crisps and press in lightly.

Cut the pastry into fingers about 3 inches long and ½ inch wide.
Place on dampened baking sheets.

Bake in a moderately hot oven, gas mark 6, 400° F., for 15 minutes, or until pastry is well puffed and cooked through.

Serve warm or cold as canapés.

Makes about 45.

EASY EGGS BENEDICT

Preparation Time: 10 minutes · Cooking Time: NIL

4 thin slices ham
4 eggs
10½ oz. can condensed cream
of chicken, mushroom or
celery soup

3-6 tablespoons milk
Little butter
4 slices buttered toast
1 tablespoon chopped parsley

Melt a little butter in a frying pan and fry the ham slices lightly
on both sides. Keep warm.

Bring ½ inch water and 1 tablespoon vinegar to simmering point
in a shallow pan. Break in the eggs and poach until cooked
to taste.

Blend the soup and milk in a saucepan and bring to boiling
point.

Place a slice of ham on each piece of toast. Top with a poached
egg and spoon the sauce over the eggs.

Serve sprinkled with chopped parsley.

GARLIC BREAD

Preparation Time: 10 minutes · Cooking Time: 20-25 minutes

Small French loaf   2 cloves garlic (crushed)
4 oz. butter

Slice the loaf deeply but don't cut right through.
Cream butter with the garlic and spread on both sides of the
    bread slices.
Wrap in foil and heat through in a moderate oven, gas mark 4,
350° F., for 20-25 minutes.

HAM AND CHEESE TOASTS

Preparation Time: 10 minutes · Cooking Time: NIL

2 slices buttered toast   2 slices processed Cheddar
1¼ oz. jar ham spread   cheese

Cover toast with ham spread.
Cut cheese into strips and arrange in a lattice pattern on ham.
Place under a hot grill for a few seconds until cheese melts and
    turns golden.

HAM AND PINEAPPLE RAREBIT

Preparation Time: 10 minutes · Cooking Time: NIL

4 slices white bread   2 oz. grated Cheddar cheese
6 oz. sliced cooked ham   Salt and pepper
4 canned or fresh pineapple
    rings

Using a plain pastry cutter about the size of the pineapple rings,
    cut 4 circles from the slices of white bread.
Now cut 4 circles from the ham.
Toast the bread lightly on both sides, cover each piece with a
    slice of ham and a well-drained pineapple ring.
Top with a thick covering of grated cheese. Season with salt and
    pepper.
Place under a hot grill until cheese is bubbling and brown.
Serve on hot plates.

KIPPER PÂTÉ CANAPÉS

Preparation Time: 10 minutes · Cooking Time: NIL

7 oz. can kipper fillets
1 tablespoon soured cream
2 hardboiled eggs
1 teaspoon chopped parsley

Salt and pepper
Plain biscuits, toast or pieces
of celery

Drain kippers and remove skin. Mash well.
Remove shells from hardboiled eggs and chop finely.
Combine kipper fillets, hardboiled eggs, sourced cream and
parsley.
Blend with a fork and add seasoning to taste.
Pipe or spread the pâté onto the biscuits, toast or pieces of celery.
If piping the mixture, make sure that the eggs are chopped very
finely and the kippers mashed thoroughly. If not, the piping
tube will block.

RAJAH'S RAREBIT

Preparation Time: 10 minutes · Cooking Time: NIL

Two 4 oz. packets cream cheese
4 slices granary bread

4 dessertspoons mango chutney
Butter

Place the cheese in a saucepan over a low heat, stirring from
time to time till melted. Add a knob of butter.
Toast the bread lightly on both sides and spread with butter on
one side, then mango chutney.
Spoon over the melted cheese and place under the grill for a
few seconds to brown slightly.
Serve at once.

SARDINE TOAST

Preparation Time: 10 minutes · Cooking Time: NIL

2 oz. butter
3 oz. fresh breadcrumbs
2 hardboiled eggs

4½ oz. can sardines
Salt and pepper
Buttered toast

Melt butter in pan and add breadcrumbs.

When heated, add chopped hardboiled eggs, drained mashed
  sardines.

Season.

Pile onto buttered toast, grill until golden brown.

SPICED FRANKFURTERS

Preparation Time: 10 minutes · Cooking Time: NIL

6 frankfurters	1 tablespoon prepared mustard
1 oz. butter	6 long soft rolls
4 tablespoons tomato ketchup	

Fry the frankfurters gently in butter until lightly browned.

Combine the ketchup and mustard and add to the frying pan.

Cook over a low heat, turning frankfurters in the sauce until
  well coated (about 2-3 minutes).

Serve each frankfurter in split, toasted roll.

SUPPERTIME SAVOURY

Preparation Time: 10 minutes · Cooking Time: NIL

4 large slices bread	¼ teaspoon Worcestershire
1 oz. butter	sauce
1 teaspoon prepared mustard	6 oz. grated Cheddar cheese
¼ teaspoon salt	2 tablespoons evaporated milk
Pinch cayenne pepper	2 tomatoes

Toast the bread on one side only.

Cream together the softened butter, mustard, salt, cayenne
  pepper and Worcestershire sauce. Add the grated cheese and
  evaporated milk and mix well.

Spread equal amounts thickly over the untoasted sides of the
  bread.

Place under a hot grill to brown.

Serve at once garnished with quartered tomatoes.

15 minutes

BAKED FRANKFURTERS IN BREAD

Preparation Time: 15 minutes · Cooking Time: 15 minutes

White bread
Frankfurters
Mustard

Chutney
Melted butter

Allow one slice of bread to each frankfurter.

Remove the crusts from the bread slices, making sure that the slices are long enough to wrap round the frankfurters and overlap slightly (to secure easily).

Spread each bread slice with a little mustard and chutney.

Wrap a piece of bread round each frankfurter, secure ends with cocktail sticks or small metal skewers. Brush with melted butter.

Place on a baking sheet and cook at gas mark 7, 425° F., for 15 minutes, or until the bread is crisp and golden.

BANANA AND BACON STICKS

Preparation Time: 15 minutes · Cooking Time: NIL

8 rashers streaky bacon
8 small bananas
Juice of 1 lemon

Pineapple jam
Watercress

Remove rinds from the bacon and peel the bananas. Dip the bananas in lemon juice.

Wrap a rasher of bacon round each banana and secure with cocktail sticks.

Place under a moderate grill until light golden-brown and crisp.

Heat pineapple jam with the remaining lemon juice and serve in a small jug or poured over the rolls. Garnish with watercress.

CHEESE AND SALMON BUNS

Preparation Time: 15 minutes · Cooking Time: 20-30 minutes

1 heaped tablespoonful dried milk powder	Pinch cayenne pepper
6 oz. self-raising flour	3 oz. butter or margarine
¼ teaspoon baking powder	2 oz. grated cheese
½ teaspoon salt	3½ oz. can salmon
½ teaspoon dry mustard	1 standard egg

Reconstitute the dried milk powder by mixing it with 6 tablespoons cold water.

Sift together the flour, baking powder, and seasonings into a bowl.

Rub in the fat until the mixture resembles fine breadcrumbs.

Stir in the grated cheese and drained and flaked fish.

Mix to a soft dough with the beaten egg and the milk.

Divide the mixture among 12 greased, deep bun tins and bake in a moderately hot oven, gas mark 6, 400° F., for 20-30 minutes or until cooked.

Remove from tins and cool on a wire rack.

Serve with butter, or, for a quick lunch, eat with salad.

CHEESE AND SARDINE ROLLS

Preparation Time: 15 minutes · Cooking Time: 15 minutes

4 oz. plain flour	2 oz. grated cheese
Salt	4½ oz. can sardines in tomato
Little cayenne	sauce
2 oz. butter or margarine	

Sift flour, salt and cayenne into a bowl. Rub in the butter or margarine until the mixture resembles fine breadcrumbs. Add the cheese and mix to a soft dough with water.

Roll out on a lightly-floured board to a rectangle 12 inches by 9 inches.

Mash the sardines with a fork. Spread lightly across the pastry, then cut into 3-inch squares.

Form each square into a roll and place on a baking sheet.

Brush with beaten egg or milk and bake in a moderately hot

oven, gas mark 6, 400° F., for 15 minutes or until golden and cooked through.

These rolls are nicest served warm.

CHEESE FINGERS

Preparation Time: 15 minutes · Cooking Time: NIL

½ lb. Esrom or Port Salut cheese
Beaten egg

Browned breadcrumbs
Oil for deep frying

Cut the cheese into flat slices ¾ inch thick.

Cut the slices into fingers ½ inch wide and about 3 inches long.

Brush the cheese fingers with beaten egg and coat with bread-crumbs.

Press the breadcrumbs gently with the flat of knife and shake off the excess.

Keep cool until needed.

To serve: Deep fry the fingers for 2-3 minutes.

EGGS IN POTATO

Preparation Time: 15 minutes · Cooking Time: 10 minutes

3-4 serving packet instant mashed potato
1 oz. butter

3 eggs
Salt and pepper

Make up the potato as directed and add the butter.

Place the mixture in a piping bag and pipe the potato into 3 circles, building up the sides. Or the nests may be moulded, using a spoon.

Bake in a moderate oven, gas mark 5, 375° F., for 5 minutes.

Remove from the oven, drop an egg into the well of each nest and sprinkle with salt and pepper. Return to the oven for 10 minutes or until eggs are cooked to taste.

Serves 3.

FIREWORK PIZZAS

Preparation Time: 15 minutes · Cooking Time: NIL

1 onion
1 oz. butter
4 oz. ham
3 tablespoons tomato pickle

9 cooked pastry cases, about 3
  inches in diameter
2 oz. finely grated cheese
Stuffed olives
1¾ oz. can anchovy fillets

Peel and chop the onion. Sauté in the butter until transparent.
Add the ham cut into small dice, then stir in the tomato pickle.
Place the pastry cases on a baking sheet and spoon some ham
  mixture into each one. Sprinkle a line of grated cheese across
  the centre of each pizza.
Heat through in a moderately hot oven, gas mark 6, 400° F.,
  for 5 minutes.
Halve 10 olives and wrap a trimmed anchovy round each one.
Garnish each pizza with one of these.
Serve hot.

FRIED SCALLOPS WITH BACON

Preparation Time: 15 minutes · Cooking Time: NIL

8 oz. packet frozen scallops
1 egg
Browned breadcrumbs

8 rashers smoked streaky bacon
Oil for deep frying

Thaw the scallops. Dip into beaten egg and roll in breadcrumbs.
Fry in deep oil until golden brown and cooked through—
  about 5 minutes.
Drain on absorbent paper. While scallops are cooking, remove
  rinds from bacon, halve rashers lengthwise, and fry until
  crisp.
Wrap half a bacon rasher round each scallop and secure with
  cocktail sticks.

PIZZA GRILL SANDWICHES
Preparation Time: 15 minutes · Cooking Time NIL

6 oz. can tomato purée	24 slices white bread
¼ cup water	24 slices processed cheese
1 teaspoon oregano	Butter

Mix first 3 ingredients for pizza sauce.

Place a slice of cheese on a slice of bread, spread pizza sauce over and top with a second slice of cheese.

Cover with a second slice of bread. Brush outside of bread with butter.

Grill on both sides until cheese begins to melt and bread is toasted.

Makes 12 sandwiches.

POACHED EGGS SUPREME
Preparation Time: 15 minutes · Cooking Time NIL

1 medium onion	5 tablespoons milk
1 oz. butter	4 eggs
10½ oz. can condensed cream of chicken soup	4 rounds of bread
Salt and pepper	Extra butter
Nutmeg	Parsley

Cook chopped or grated onion in butter until soft but not brown.

Stir in soup, milk and seasoning. Heat gently.

Poach eggs.

Toast bread: butter.

Place an egg on each slice of bread, and spoon the sauce over each.

Chop the parsley and sprinkle it on the top.

SAVOURY POPOVERS
(to go with roast beef)
Preparation Time: 15 minutes · Cooking Time: 20 minutes

2 teaspoons dried onion flakes
Water (amount as given on
batter mix packet)

1 egg
4½ oz. packet batter mix

Soak onions in the water for 10 minutes, then use the water
(plus onions) and the egg to make up mix as directed.
Bake in individual greased patty tins in a hot oven for 20
minutes till golden-brown.

SPINACH AND BACON TOAST
Preparation Time: 15 minutes · Cooking Time: NIL

2 rashers bacon
5½ oz. packet frozen chopped
spinach
Salt, pepper, and grated nutmeg

1 egg
Little butter
2 slices toast
1 tomato

De-rind the bacon and cut into small pieces. Fry lightly.
Cook spinach according to packet instruction. Add the bacon.
Season with salt, pepper and nutmeg.
Beat the egg, add to spinach and cook over a low heat, stirring
continuously, until the mixture begins to thicken. Butter
the toast and pile the spinach onto the 2 slices.
Garnish with slices of tomato and serve at once.
Serves 2.

TURKEY AND HAM SAVOURIES
Preparation Time: 15 minutes · Cooking Time NIL

4 slices white bread
Dripping or butter for frying
4 slices ham

4 thin slices cooked turkey
breast
¼ pint parsley sauce

Remove the crusts from the bread and fry the slices in dripping or butter until golden on both sides. Remove from pan and drain on absorbent paper. Keep warm.

Quickly fry the slices of ham in the remaining fat and put a slice on each piece of fried bread.

Top with a slice of turkey and coat with a little hot parsley sauce.

Serve at once.

20 minutes

HOT KIPPER LOAF

Preparation Time: 20 minutes · Cooking Time: 15 minutes

6 oz. packet frozen kipper fillets
2 oz. butter

1 dessertspoon lemon juice
Salt and pepper
French loaf

Cook kipper fillets according to instructions on packet.

Drain, remove skin and flake flesh.

Pound together kippers, softened butter, lemon juice, and seasoning

Cut French loaf into inch thick slices, to within ½ inch of the bottom of the loaf. Press a little of the kipper mixture between each slice, reform the loaf and wrap in foil.

Bake in a moderately hot oven, gas mark 6, 400° F., for 15 minutes.

Serve hot.

KIPPER TARTLETS

Preparation Time: 20 minutes · Cooking Time: NIL

7½ oz. packet frozen but thawed shortcrust pastry
7 oz. packet kipper fillets
½ pint packet white sauce mix
⅓ pint milk

2 hardboiled eggs
Juice of 1 lemon
Salt and pepper
Chopped parsley

Roll out thawed pastry thinly on a lightly-floured board.

Cut out 12 rounds with a 3½-inch plain cutter and line into

patty tins. Prick bases with a fork and bake in a hot oven, gas mark 7, 425° F., for about 15 minutes or until golden-brown.

Meanwhile, cook the kippers according to the instructions on the packet, then skin and flake.

Make up the white sauce according to directions but using only ⅓ pint milk.

Remove shells from hard-boiled eggs and chop. Add to white sauce together with the flaked fish, lemon juice and seasoning.

Fill the pastry cases with this mixture, and garnish with chopped parsley.

Serve hot or cold.

PÂTÉ AND BACON ROLLS

Preparation Time: 20 minutes · Cooking Time: NIL

8 oz. smoked rindless back bacon	1 tablespoon chopped parsley
4 oz. liver pâté	Squeeze lemon juice
3 oz. white breadcrumbs	Salt and pepper

Spread each rasher flat with the back of a knife.

Cut in half crosswise.

Place liver pâté in a basin with breadcrumbs and parsley and mix well together, adding a squeeze of lemon juice and seasoning to taste.

Spread each piece of bacon with a little of the stuffing and roll up.

Don't overfill the rolls, the stuffing will fall out.

Secure with a cocktail stick.

Cook under a hot grill for 10 minutes, turning occasionally until lightly browned and crisp.

Serve hot.

PICKLED POTATOBURGERS

Preparation Time: 20 minutes · Cooking Time: NIL

5 oz. packet crispy fry potato
    mix
2 oz. finely grated cheese or 2
    teaspoons grated onion
1 teaspoon salt

Pepper
¼ teaspoon paprika pepper
Pickle
Oil for deep frying

Make up the potato mix as directed on packet, using water.
    Stir in the cheese or onion and the seasonings.
Roll out the potato mixture on a floured board until about
    ¼-inch thick. Cut into 2-inch circles with a pastry cutter.
    Put a little pickle onto half the circles. Dampen the edges
    with water and top with another circle of potato. Seal edges
    well.
Deep fry in hot oil until golden-brown; drain on absorbent
    paper.
Serve hot with a green salad.

PIPÉRADE

Preparation Time: 20 minutes · Cooking Time: NIL

3 oz. butter
1 onion
14 oz. can tomatoes
2 roasted pimentos

Salt and pepper
Pinch thyme
6 eggs
Buttered toast

Heat 2 oz. butter and fry the chopped onion until tender with-
    out allowing it to colour.
Add tomatoes and sliced pimentos and heat gently. Season
    well, add the thyme, cover and cook for 5 minutes.
In another pan, heat rest of the butter. Pour in the beaten
    eggs and cook, stirring lightly, over a gentle heat until the
    egg is almost set.
Fold the vegetable mixture into the eggs, but do not try to
    mix thoroughly.
When firm, turn onto a dish and serve immediately with hot
    buttered toast.
(You can omit the toast and serve the pipérade topped with
    grilled bacon rashers.)

25 minutes

PINEAPPLE AND BACON DECKERS
Preparation Time: 25 minutes · Cooking Time: NIL

15 oz. can pineapple rings	Browned breadcrumbs
8 oz. streaky bacon	Oil for frying
White bread	Watercress
1 beaten egg	

Drain the pineapple rings, reserving the syrup.

Remove rinds from the bacon. Flatten the rashers, using a round-bladed knife, and cut each in half across the middle. Form each rasher into rolls and grill gently until cooked to taste, turning once during cooking.

Using a pastry cutter the same size as the pineapple rings, cut rounds of bread from slices ½-inch thick, allowing 1 piece bread to each pineapple round.

Dip the bread rounds quickly into the reserved pineapple syrup. Coat with beaten egg and breadcrumbs.

Heat ½-inch oil in a frying-pan. Test when hot enough with a small piece of bread—if oil sizzles round edges of bread, it is the right heat.

Fry the coated bread rounds until golden, turning them once. Drain on absorbent paper and keep warm.

Meanwhile, heat the pineapple rings under the grill, but do not allow them to brown.

To serve: Place a pineapple ring on each round of fried bread. Arrange on a heated serving plate and top with bacon rolls. Garnish with watercress and serve immediately.

Main Courses

Main Courses – 5 minutes

BAKED HAM
Preparation Time: 5 minutes · Cooking Time: 20 minutes

2 lb. can of ham
Brown sugar
Cloves

8½ oz. can of crushed pineapple, drained

Put ham into a baking tin. Sprinkle brown sugar over it and
stick in cloves.
Cover the ham with the pineapple.
Bake at gas mark 6, 400° F., for about 20 minutes.

QUICK TURKEY SUPREME
Preparation Time: 5 minutes · Cooking Time: 30 minutes

10 oz. packet turkey breasts
16 oz. packet mixed frozen
vegetables
11½ oz. can sweetcorn

10½ oz. can condensed chicken
or mushroom soup
Small amount of butter

Place all the ingredients in a casserole. Cook for ½ hour at
gas mark 6, 400° F.
(Serve with instant mashed potato or quick-cooking rice.)

10 minutes

AMERICAN SALMON DISH
Preparation Time: 10 minutes · Cooking Time: NIL

1 oz. butter
½ green pepper
7½ oz. can salmon
11 oz. can cream-style corn

Worcestershire sauce
Salt and pepper
2-3 serving packet instant
mashed potato

Melt the butter in a saucepan.
Remove seeds and pith from pepper and cut into thin strips.
Add to pan, cover, and cook slowly for 5 minutes or until
soft.

Remove skin and bones from salmon, flake flesh and add with its liquor to the saucepan.

Stir in the creamed corn and salt, pepper and Worcestershire sauce to taste.

Bring to simmering point and add a little milk if necessary.

Meanwhile, make up the potato according to directions on pack and pipe a border of potato round the edge of the serving dish.

Spoon the salmon into the centre.

APRICOT GLAZED HAM

Preparation Time: 10 minutes · Cooking Time: 55 minutes

2 lb. canned ham	1 teaspoon dry mustard
15 oz. can apricot halves	1 tablespoon dry sherry
4 oz. soft brown sugar	

Remove excess jelly from ham. Place ham in a small roasting tin.

Drain the apricots, reserving 4 tablespoons syrup for the glaze.

Mix together the sugar, mustard and sherry. Moisten with the reserved apricot syrup.

Pour this glaze over the ham and roast in a moderately hot oven, gas mark 6, 400° F., for 45 minutes, basting occasionally. At the end of this time, arrange the apricot halves on top of the ham, coat with glaze and return to the oven for a further 10 minutes.

Serve hot or cold, decorated with halved glacé cherries.

BRISLING GRATINÉE

Preparation Time: 10 minutes · Cooking Time: 15-20 minutes

Two 3¾ oz. cans brisling in tomato sauce	A pinch of basil
8 oz. can peeled tomatoes	Salt and pepper
A good squeeze lemon juice	3 tablespoons breadcrumbs
1 dessertspoon instant onion	½ oz. butter

Put the brisling in a shallow ovenproof dish.

Mix together the tomatoes, onion, basil, lemon juice and seasoning.

Cover the fish with this mixture.

Scatter the breadcrumbs over the top and dot with butter.

Bake in a moderately hot oven, gas mark 6, 400° F., for 15-20 minutes until the top is nicely browned.

If preferred, this dish can be made in 4 scallop shells and a border of instant mashed potato piped round the edge of each shell.

After 5 minutes in the oven, remove, brush with beaten egg and return to oven to brown.

CELERY THING

Preparation Time: 10 minutes · Cooking Time: 25-30 minutes

Two 14 oz. cans celery hearts	2 tablespoons sage and onion
3 oz. cheese	stuffing mix
15¼ oz. can oxtail soup	4 tablespoons boiling water

Butter an ovenproof dish and arrange drained celery hearts in base.

Grate the cheese and dot the celery with most of it. Pour soup over.

Mix together the stuffing mix and boiling water.

Dot it over the soup with the remainder of the cheese.

Bake at gas mark 6, 400° F., for 25-30 minutes.

Good on its own, or with sausages or grilled ham.

CHEESE AND ONION SUPPER DISH

Preparation Time: 10 minutes · Cooking Time: 25 minutes

4 oz. white breadcrumbs	Salt and pepper
4 tomatoes	15 oz. can consommé
1 clove garlic	1 tablespoon instant onion
4 oz. grated cheese	flakes

Arrange alternate layers of breadcrumbs, peeled and sliced tomatoes, grated cheese and seasoning in a heat-proof dish.

Crush garlic with a little salt.

Stir garlic into the consommé with the onion flakes (heat gently in a saucepan if the soup has jellied). Pour into dish.

Bake in a moderate oven, gas mark 5, 375° F., for 25 minutes.

Serve hot.

CHILI CON CARNE

Preparation Time: 10 minutes · Cooking Time: 10 minutes

15½ oz. can red beans
15½ oz. can minced steak
8 oz. can tomatoes
2¼ oz. can tomato purée
¼ teaspoon instant garlic
   powder

1 sachet bouquet garni
1 teaspoon compound chili
   powder, or to taste
1 dessertspoon Worcestershire
   sauce
Salt and pepper

Drain red beans if packed in brine.
Combine ingredients in a pan and simmer for 10 minutes.

EGGS TUNATO

Preparation Time: 10 minutes · Cooking Time: 20 minutes

2-3 serving packet instant
   mashed potato
7 oz. can tuna steak
8 oz. can tomatoes

Chili powder to taste
4 eggs
4 fl. oz. carton single cream

Make up the mashed potato according to directions on packet.
   Fill into a piping bag and pipe a border round the sides of
   a buttered, shallow, ovenproof dish.
Drain and flake the tuna, mix with the tomatoes and chili
   powder to taste.
Spread across base of dish.
Break the eggs onto the tuna mixture and pour over the cream.
Bake in a moderately hot oven, gas mark 6, 400° F., for 20
   minutes or until eggs are set.

FARMER'S CHEESE DISH

Preparation Time: 10 minutes · Cooking Time: 20 minutes

8 slices white bread
2 oz. butter
½ lb. Nökkelost cheese (spiced
   Norwegian cheese)

4 eggs
¼ pint milk
Salt and pepper
Chopped chives

Spread the bread slices with butter. Remove crusts.

Cut the cheese into 8 slices and place one on each piece of bread. Halve slices diagonally.

Arrange, overlapping, in a buttered, shallow, heatproof dish.

Combine beaten eggs, milk and seasoning. Pour over bread and cheese.

Bake in a moderate oven, gas mark 4, 350° F., for 20 minutes, or until egg mixture has set.

Then brown bread quickly under a hot grill.

Serve sprinkled with chopped chives.

FORCEMEAT CHICKEN BAKE

Preparation Time: 10 minutes · Cooking Time: 25 minutes

4 oz. fresh breadcrumbs	Salt and pepper
1½ oz. prepared suet	1 egg
1 tablespoon chopped parsley	2 tablespoons milk
Pinch of thyme	7¼ oz. can chicken supreme
Little grated onion or lemon rind	

Mix together the breadcrumbs, suet, herbs, lemon rind or onion and seasoning, then bind with the egg and milk. Use about two-thirds of this mixture to line the bottom and sides of a ¾-1 pint pie dish.

Turn the contents of the can of chicken into the lined dish and cover with the remaining forcemeat, patted over the surface.

Bake in a hot oven, gas mark 7, 425° F., for 25 minutes.

Serve with green vegetables.

HAM AND PEACH ROLLS

Preparation Time: 10 minutes · Cooking Time: 20 minutes

8 oz. Cheddar cheese	Salt and pepper
8 slices ham	Little grated nutmeg
11 oz. can creamed sweetcorn	15 oz. can peach halves
2 tablespoons milk	Parsley

Cut cheese into 8 fingers.

Place one on each ham slice and roll up.

Place rolls in a shallow greased ovenproof dish.

Stir milk, salt, pepper and nutmeg into sweetcorn and spoon over middle of rolls.

Drain the peach halves and arrange down sides or at ends of dish. Bake in a moderately hot oven, gas mark 6, 400° F., for 10 minutes, or until heated through and cheese has softened.

Serve garnished with parsley and accompanied by boiled rice or mashed potatoes.

HAM ROLL-UPS

Preparation Time: 10 minutes · Cooking Time: NIL

8 oz. can pineapple pieces	¼ teaspoon salt
3 sticks celery	1 teaspoon lemon juice
Two 3 oz. packets cream cheese	8 slices ham

Drain the pineapple.

Chop the celery finely.

Blend together the cream cheese, salt, lemon juice and celery.

Spread each slice of ham with this mixture.

Heap a tablespoon of crushed pineapple across one end of each ham slice. Roll up and chill.

Serve on tossed green salad with buttered new potatoes.

HOT TUNA PIE

Preparation Time: 10 minutes · Cooking Time: 20-25 minutes

6½ oz. can savoury tuna	½ pint packet white sauce mix
7½ oz. can button mushrooms	½ pint milk
1 dessertspoon Worcestershire sauce	¼ pint mayonnaise
1 tablespoon vinegar	17½ oz. can diced potatoes
	Standard packet potato crisps

Combine tuna, drained mushrooms, Worcestershire sauce and vinegar.

Make up white sauce using the milk. Remove from heat and allow to cool slightly before stirring in mayonnaise. Season well.

Place half the drained potatoes in base of ovenproof dish.

Add half the tuna mixture. Repeat with remaining potatoes and tuna.

Pour over prepared sauce. Top with potato crisps. Bake in a moderate oven, gas mark 4, 350° F., for 20-25 minutes.

Serve hot, preferably with grilled tomatoes or with a green salad.

This dish can be prepared in advance, then topped with crisps and baked before serving.

ISLANDS TUNA CURRY

Preparation Time: 10 minutes · Cooking Time: NIL

1 oz. butter or ghee	1 oz. creamed coconut
1 dessertspoon curry powder	Two 4½ oz. cans tuna
½ teaspoon instant garlic	¼ pint tomato juice
1 teaspoon instant onion	Salt

Melt the butter or ghee in a saucepan, add the curry powder and fry for a minute.

Add tomato juice, instant onion, instant garlic and the chopped creamed coconut.

Simmer, uncovered, until the coconut has melted.

Stir in the drained and flaked tuna to heat through, and add salt to taste.

If a hotter curry is preferred, add a sliced fresh green chili or ½ teaspoon chili powder.

Serve with a savoury or plain boiled rice.

LACTIC CHEESE FONDUE

Preparation Time: 10 minutes · Cooking Time: NIL

4 4½ oz. packets lactic cheese spread	1 wineglass dry white wine French bread

Place cheese and wine in a saucepan and heat gently, stirring, until the mixture is quite smooth.

Do not allow it to become over-heated and add more wine if necessary to obtain the correct coating consistency.

Serve in an ovenproof dish over a table heater.

Hand round crusty French bread and provide fondue forks (or ordinary forks or skewers) to make the dipping easier.

NEWBURG PRAWNS

Preparation Time: 10 minutes · Cooking Time: NIL

8 oz. quick-cooking rice	2 egg yolks
6 oz. can prawns	¼ pint single cream
1 oz. butter	Salt and cayenne pepper
3 tablespoons sherry	Chopped parsley

Cook rice as directed on packet.

While it is cooking, rinse and drain the prawns and heat very gently in the butter for a minute.

Add sherry and cook for a further 2 minutes.

Blend egg yolks and cream, pour into the prawn mixture and add seasoning to taste.

Heat, gently stirring, until mixture thickens. Do not boil.

Serve on the rice, garnished with parsley.

PIZZA OMELETTE

Preparation Time: 10 minutes · Cooking Time: NIL

3 oz. Cheddar cheese	2 tablespoons water
4 oz. lean ham	1 teaspoon mixed herbs
2 tomatoes	3 tablespoons tomato ketchup
1 oz. butter	Salt and pepper
6 eggs	

Cut the cheese into thin slices; chop the ham, skin and slice the tomatoes.

Beat the eggs with the water and add salt and pepper.

Pre-heat the grill.

Heat a large omelette pan, add the butter and, when sizzling, add the beaten eggs.

Cook the omelette in the usual way until the base is firm but the top still moist. Quickly cover with ham and tomato ketchup and sprinkle with the mixed herbs, if used.

Arrange sliced tomato and cheese on top.

Place the omelette under the heated grill and leave until cheese is golden brown—about 1-2 minutes.

Slide the omelette out of pan onto a serving-dish and serve immediately.

RAVIOLI SPECIAL

Preparation Time: 10 minutes · Cooking Time: 30 minutes

16 oz. can ravioli ½ green pepper
4 tomatoes 4 oz. cheese

Put ravioli in an ovenproof dish. Top with sliced pepper and
sliced tomato.
Grate the cheese and sprinkle it on top.
Bake at gas mark 4, 350° F., for ½ hour.

SARDINE SUPPER

Preparation Time: 10 minutes · Cooking Time: 20 minutes

1 lb. 3 oz. can potatoes ½ pint milk
4½ oz. can sardines 2 tablespoons crushed potato
1 packet white sauce mix crisps

Drain potatoes and slice thinly.
Arrange half in a buttered 1½ pint ovenproof dish.
Place drained sardines on top.
Cover with remaining potatoes.
Make up white sauce.
Pour over, and top with crushed crisps.
Cook in a moderately hot oven, gas mark 6, 400° F., for 20
minutes till browned.
Serves 2 to 3.

SAUERKRAUT AND FRANKFURTERS

Preparation Time: 10 minutes · Cooking Time: 15 minutes

14 oz. can sauerkraut ¼ teaspoon ground caraway
8 oz. can frankfurters seeds
2 rashers streaky bacon Bayleaf

Dice de-rinded bacon rashers.
Fry gently 2 to 3 minutes.
Stir in sauerkraut and herbs, then add drained frankfurters.
Cover and simmer 10 minutes.

SAVOURY CRUMBLE

Preparation Time: 10 minutes · Cooking Time: 30 minutes

15½ oz. can minced steak and
   onion in gravy
2¼ oz. can tomato purée
2 oz. butter

4 oz. plain flour
4 oz. grated Cheddar cheese
Pinch salt and pepper

Heat the minced steak gently in a saucepan and stir in the
   tomato purée.
Spread meat mixture in the base of a large, fairly shallow oven-
   proof dish.
Sift the flour and salt into a bowl.
Add a little pepper and rub in the butter. Add the grated
   cheese.
Cover the meat with the crumble mixture.
Bake at gas mark 5, 375° F., for 30 minutes.
The crumble can be used to top other savoury mixes.

SAVOURY SALMON PICNIC LOAF

Preparation Time: 10 minutes · Cooking Time: 1 hour

15½ oz. can salmon
2 oz. fresh breadcrumbs
4 gherkins
½ teaspoon basil
½ teaspoon parsley flakes
¼ teaspoon dry mustard

½ teaspoon pepper lemon
   seasoning
2 tablespoons instant minced
   onion
2 eggs
6 fluid ounces milk

Drain the salmon, remove skin and bone and flake flesh.
Place in a basin with the breadcrumbs, chopped gherkins, herbs,
   onion and seasonings.
Mix well and bind with beaten eggs, milk, melted butter and
   lemon juice.
Turn into a greased loaf tin and bake in a moderate oven, gas
   mark 4, 350° F., for 1 hour or until loaf is delicately golden,
   firm and tender. Turn out.
Serve cold, cut into slices.

TOMATO BEEF BAKE

Preparation Time: 10 minutes · Cooking Time: 25-30 minutes

7 oz. can corned beef
10 oz. can garden peas
10½ oz. can condensed tomato
  rice soup

2-3 serving packet instant
  mashed potato
1 oz. butter
Salt and pepper

Remove corned beef from can and cut into slices. Arrange
  then in base of ovenproof dish.
Season and cover with the drained peas.
Spread the undiluted soup over the top.
Make up the mashed potato following directions on the packet.
  Add the butter and seasoning to taste. Spread potato lightly
  across top of dish. Decorate with a fork.
Bake in a moderately hot oven, gas mark 6, 400° F., for 25-30
  minutes, or until well-heated and potato browned.

15 minutes

ASPARAGUS SAVOURY

Preparation Time: 15 minutes · Cooking Time: NIL

12 oz. can of whole asparagus
½ pint packet white sauce mix

4 eggs
Salt and pepper

Drain the asparagus and put into an ovenproof dish.
Make up the white sauce as directed on the packet and pour it
  over the asparagus.
Make 4 indentations in the sauce and break 1 egg into each.
Season.
Bake in a moderate oven, gas mark 3, 350° F., until the eggs
  are lightly set.
(This is very good, too, if some ham is put in the dish before
  the asparagus goes in. The eggs can also be topped with
  grated cheese before baking.)

BACON AND CORNED BEEF MEAT CAKES

Preparation Time: 15 minutes · Cooking Time: 20-25 minutes

1 small onion	7 oz. can corned beef
1 oz. dripping or bacon fat	Salt and pepper
2-3 serving packet instant	1 egg yolk
mashed potato	3 rashers streaky bacon

Peel and chop the onion. Fry in the dripping until transparent.

Make up the potato following directions on packet.

Mash the corned beef and mix with the potato and onion; season well and stir in the egg yolk.

Using floured hands, shape the mixture into 6 patties about 1 inch in depth.

Halve the de-rinded bacon rashers lengthwise and wrap one round each patty and secure with a cocktail stick.

Put onto an ovenproof dish and bake in a fairly hot oven, gas mark 6, 400° F., for 20-25 minutes or until bacon is brown and crisp.

Serve with grilled tomatoes.

Serves 3.

BACON AND ONION GRILL

Preparation Time: 15 minutes · Cooking Time: NIL

5 oz. packet frozen button	Medium can garden peas
onions in sauce	Salt and pepper
4 oz. cheese	4 rashers bacon

Heat onions according to directions on packet, then remove from heat.

Grate the cheese and add 3 oz. of it to the onions. Add the peas but not the liquid. Season.

Cut bacon into small pieces and fry or grill until crisp.

Drain and add to onion mixture.

Pour into a shallow ovenproof dish.

Sprinkle remainder of grated cheese on top. Grill until cheese melts.

BANANA CURRY

Preparation Time: 15 minutes · Cooking Time: 10 minutes

½ pint packet curry sauce mix
½ pint chicken stock
1 apple

4 bananas
2 oz. butter
2 oz. creamed coconut

Combine the sauce mix and stock in a saucepan. Bring to the boil and simmer for 5 minutes.

Meanwhile, peel, core and chop the apple roughly.

Peel the bananas and cut into quarters.

Melt the butter in a frying-pan and cook the bananas gently for about 5 minutes, turning them once.

Add the chopped creamed coconut to the sauce and stir until dissolved.

Add the bananas and apple and simmer, covered, for 10 minutes.

Serve with boiled rice.

BEAN STEW

Preparation Time: 15 minutes · Cooking Time: NIL

1 large onion
1 oz. butter
10½ oz. can mulligatawny soup
10½ oz. can vegetable soup
2 oz. peeled prawns

7¾ oz. can baked beans and frankfurters
1 small can sweetcorn
6 oz. cooked ham
1 oz. grated cheese
Chopped chives

Peel and slice the onion. Sauté in the butter over a gentle heat until transparent.

Add the mulligatawny soup and the vegetable soup, with the drained rinsed prawns, baked beans and frankfurters, the drained sweetcorn and the ham, cut into 1-inch cubes; heat thoroughly.

Transfer to a heated serving dish and top with grated cheese and chopped chives.

BEEF AND MACARONI CASSEROLE

Preparation Time: 15 minutes · Cooking Time: 30 minutes

4 oz. quick-cooking macaroni
15½ oz. can minced beef
4 oz. packet frozen but thawed
  peas
Salt and pepper

2-3 serving packet instant
  mashed potato
2 tomatoes
Beaten egg or milk

Cook macaroni in boiling salted water as directed on packet; drain.

Place half the minced beef in a well-greased ovenproof dish, top with thawed peas and cooked macaroni. Season.

Place remaining minced beef on top.

Make up instant potato according to directions and spread over casserole.

Brush with beaten egg or milk.

Slice the tomatoes and arrange round edge of dish.

Bake in a moderate oven, gas mark 5, 375° F., for 30 minutes.

You can vary this recipe by using other vegetables, such as frozen beans.

BEEF AND RED WINE CASSEROLE

Preparation Time: 15 minutes · Cooking Time: 20 minutes

Two 15½ oz. cans stewing steak
¼ lb. shredded bacon
2 teaspoons dried onion
1 clove garlic, crushed
Pinch dried thyme

½ bay leaf
10¼ oz. can mushroom soup
2 oz. sliced mushrooms
¼ pint Burgundy (red)

Turn the cans of meat into a saucepan. In a separate pan, lightly fry the bacon.

Add the bacon to the steak with the dried onions, garlic, thyme and bay leaf.

Stir in the mushroom soup, extra mushrooms and the wine.

Simmer for about 15-20 minutes over a very low heat.

Remove bay leaf and serve at once.

BEEFBURGER BEAN BAKE

Preparation Time: 15 minutes · Cooking Time: 20 minutes

16 oz. can baked beans in tomato sauce
1 oz. fat
8 oz. packet beefburgers

1 onion
4 oz. button mushrooms
Salt and pepper

Place the baked beans in an ovenproof dish.

Melt the fat in a frying-pan and fry the beefburgers for a few minutes on both sides. Place on top of beans.

Peel and slice the onions and cook gently for 3-4 minutes, adding more fat to frying-pan if necessary.

Slice the mushrooms, add to pan and cook with onions for about 2 minutes. Season. Drain and place on top of the beef-burgers.

Cover and bake in a moderate oven, gas mark 5, 375° F., for 15-20 minutes.

Serve with mashed potatoes.

CELERY, POTATO AND CORN PIE

Preparation Time: 15 minutes · Cooking Time: 30-35 minutes

2 small onions or 1 larger one
1 oz. butter or 2 tablespoons oil
10 oz. can new potatoes
7 oz. can sweetcorn kernels
and peppers

15 oz. can cream of celery soup
Salt and pepper
2 eggs
2 oz. grated Cheddar cheese

Peel and slice the onions and sauté in the butter or oil until transparent. Remove from heat.

Drain and slice the potatoes. Drain the sweetcorn.

Arrange the potatoes in the base of an ovenproof dish. Top with the onion. Season. Add the sweetcorn.

Beat the eggs and stir into the soup. Season. Pour this mixture over the vegetables. Top with grated cheese.

Bake in a moderate oven, gas mark 5, 375° F., for 30-35 minutes.

Serve hot.

CHEESE AND BACON SLICES
Preparation Time: 15 minutes · Cooking Time: 25 minutes

8 oz. self-raising flour
Pinch salt
4 oz. prepared suet
Water to mix

3 teaspoons made mustard
4 oz. streaky bacon
4 oz. Cheddar cheese

Sift flour and salt into a mixing bowl. Add the suet and mix
to a pliable dough with water. Divide into two, one part
being slightly larger than the other.

Roll out the larger portion on a lightly-floured board to a rectangle about 13 inches by 10 inches, and line into a shallow
baking tin, 11 inches by 8 inches.

Spread base thinly with mustard.

Remove rinds from bacon and chop rashers. Arrange over
pastry base. Grate cheese and sprinkle it over bacon. Roll
out remaining pastry to form a lid. Brush edges of pastry
case with water. Top with the lid, press edges together and
crimp.

Brush with milk.

Bake in a moderately hot oven, gas mark 6, 400° F., for 25
minutes. Cut into 8 slices. Serve hot or cold.

CHEESE AND POTATO CAKE
Preparation Time: 15 minutes · Cooking Time: 30-40 minutes

5-6 serving packet instant
mashed potato
¾ oz. unsalted butter
6 oz. Gouda cheese
2 eggs

Salt, pepper and nutmeg
Browned breadcrumbs
8 bacon rashers
3 tomatoes

Make up the instant mashed potato following directions on
the packet. While hot, beat in the butter, grated cheese, egg
yolks and seasoning to taste.

Butter a soufflé or ovenproof dish and dust out with browned
breadcrumbs.

Remove rinds from bacon rashers, form flattened rashers into
rolls and thread onto skewers. Place in a baking tin.

Beat the egg whites stiffly and fold into the potato mixture.
Transfer to prepared dish.

Bake the cake and the bacon rolls in a moderately hot oven,
gas mark 6, 400° F., for 30-40 minutes or until top is golden
and centre firm.

Serve in dish or turned out onto a plate with the bacon rolls
and sliced tomatoes.

Serves 6.

CHEESE AND SWEETCORN SAVOURY

Preparation Time: 15 minutes · Cooking Time: NIL

1½ pint packet cheese sauce
mix
8 fl. oz. milk
11 oz. can sweetcorn
Salt and pepper

¼ teaspoon dry mustard
1 tablespoon chopped parsley
Browned breadcrumbs
½ oz. grated cheese
Little butter

Make up the cheese sauce using 8 fl. oz. milk but otherwise
following directions on the packet.

Heat the sweetcorn; drain. Mix with cheese sauce adding
mustard and chopped parsley. Season.

Transfer to a heat-proof dish, sprinkle with breadcrumbs and
grated cheese and dot with butter.

Place under a hot grill and cook until surface is golden-brown
and bubbling. Serve immediately.

This dish can also be made in individual ramekin dishes.

CHEESED VEGETABLE GRILL

Preparation Time: 15 minutes · Cooking Time: NIL

Left-over vegetables (potatoes,
carrots, swedes, peas, etc.)
2-3 sausages

2 tomatoes
2 oz. mushrooms
½ pint packet cheese sauce mix

Heat the left-over food while frying the chopped sausages,
tomatoes and mushrooms.

Put all the vegetables and sausages in a heat-proof dish.

Make the cheese sauce as directed on the packet and pour over
the vegetable and sausage mixture.

Put under a medium grill for about 5 minutes or until the top is golden-brown.

(Fried bacon, ham or chicken left-overs can be used instead of the sausages.)

CHICKEN CLARIA

Preparation Time: 15 minutes · Cooking Time: NIL

1 oz. butter	6-8 oz. diced cooked chicken
1 oz. flour	8 oz. packet frozen peas
¾ pint milk, or milk and chicken stock	2 hardboiled eggs
	Bacon rolls
Salt, pepper and ground mace	Triangles of toast

Melt the butter in a saucepan over a gentle heat, stir in the flour and cook for 2-3 minutes. Gradually blend in the milk (or milk and stock mixture) off the heat. Bring to the boil stirring continuously; simmer for 3-4 minutes.

Add seasonings. Meanwhile, cook the peas in boiling, salted water; drain.

Add the chicken and peas to the sauce, simmer for 3 minutes.

Shell the hardboiled eggs and cut into slices. Add to sauce and simmer for further 2 minutes.

Adjust the seasoning and serve garnished with grilled bacon rolls and triangles of toast.

Serves 3.

CHICKEN IN TOMATO

Preparation Time: 15 minutes · Cooking Time: 30 minutes

Oil for frying	1 pint water
4 chicken joints	4 oz. mushrooms
3-4 serving packet tomato soup	

Heat a little oil in a saucepan and add the chicken joints. Brown on both sides.

Remove the joints, add the contents of the packet of soup off the heat, blend in the water.

Stir over heat until mixture boils.

Add sliced mushrooms and replace the chicken.

Cover and simmer gently for 30 minutes, stirring from time
to time to prevent sticking.
Serve with potatoes or boiled rice.

CHICKEN LIVERS GRECO

Preparation Time: 15 minutes · Cooking Time: NIL

1 lb. chicken livers	8 oz. packet frozen green beans,
2 oz. flour	cooked
1 tablespoon salt	3 tablespoons packaged stuff-
Dash of pepper	ing mix
2 oz. butter	2 tablespoons grated Parmesan
⅛ pint chicken broth	cheese

Cut livers in half and roll the pieces in flour mixed with season-
ing.
Melt butter in frying-pan.
Add livers and sauté till lightly browned.
Add broth and simmer over low flame for 4-5 minutes.
Stir in drained cooked beans and simmer a few minutes or until
heated through.
Combine stuffing mix and grated cheese; sprinkle over in-
gredients in pan. Do not stir in.
Cover pan, turn off flame, and let it stand a few minutes or until
ready to serve. Serve hot.

CHICKEN SUPREME SOUFFLÉ

Preparation Time: 15 minutes · Cooking Time: 45 minutes

7¼ oz. can chicken supreme	1 tablespoon chopped parsley
2 eggs	Salt and pepper
7 oz. can sweetcorn	

Blend together the chicken supreme, egg yolks and drained
sweetcorn. Add the chopped parsley and seasoning. Whisk
the egg whites stiffly and fold into the chicken mixture.
Turn into a lightly-greased, 1-pint soufflé dish and stand in a
roasting tin containing hot water.
Bake in a moderate oven, gas mark 4, 350° F., for 45 minutes or
until set. Serve at once.
Serves 2.

CHICKEN WITH GRAPES

Preparation Time: 15 minutes · Cooking Time: NIL

10 oz. jar or two 5 oz. jars
  chicken fillets
Water and chicken stock
1 oz. butter
1 oz. flour
2 tablespoons dry sherry or ½
  pint dry white wine

Salt and pepper
10 oz. can grapes
5 fl. oz. carton soured cream
Little butter
1 teaspoon chopped parsley

Remove chicken fillets from jar and place in a saucepan.
Heat very gently until the jelly in which they are packed has
  melted. Strain liquid into a measuring jug. If using white
  wine, make the chicken liquid up to ¼ pint with water.
If using sherry, make the liquid up to ½ pint with a little
  chicken stock.
Melt the butter in a saucepan. Stir in the flour off the heat.
Return to heat and cook this mixture (a 'roux'), stirring all the
  time, for 2-3 minutes.
Remove, and gradually blend in the chicken liquid. Return and
  stir over heat until mixture bubbles and thickens. Simmer for
  1 minute.
Stir in the sherry or wine, 2 oz. of the drained grapes and the
  soured cream. Add the chicken. Reheat without boiling, stirring from time to time.
When the chicken is heated through, arrange on a serving dish.
Garnish with the remaining grapes which have been tossed in a
  little melted butter and chopped parsley. Serves 3.

CHICKEN WITH MUSHROOMS

Preparation Time: 15 minutes · Cooking Time: NIL

4 cooked chicken joints
2 half-pint packets white sauce
  mix
1 pint milk

7½ oz. can button mushrooms
Squeeze lemon juice
Salt and pepper
1 tablespoon chopped parsley

Remove chicken flesh from bone and cut into bite-sized pieces.
Make up white sauce, using the milk.

Drain the mushrooms and add to sauce with the chicken pieces.
Stir over a gentle heat until chicken and mushrooms are heated
through.
Season to taste with salt, pepper and a squeeze of lemon juice.
Transfer to a heated serving dish and sprinkle with chopped
parsley.
This can also be garnished with small bacon rolls.

COD CASSEROLE

Preparation Time: 15 minutes · Cooking Time: 25 minutes

One 12 oz. packet frozen cod
   steaks
Salt and pepper

½ 3-4 serving packet mushroom soup powder
¼ pint milk
½ lb. tomatoes

Place the cod steaks in a shallow fireproof dish.
Season well.
In a saucepan blend together the mushroom soup powder and
the milk. Bring to the boil, stirring occasionally. Pour over the
fish.
Slice the tomatoes and arrange on top of the fish.
Cook, covered at gas mark 4, 350° F., for 25 minutes or until the
fish is tender.
Serve with instant mashed potato.
NB. Close the soup packet down tightly. When making up the
remaining powder, remember to use a reduced amount of
liquid.

COD GRILLED WITH CHEESE

Preparation Time: 15 minutes · Cooking Time: NIL

One 12 oz. packet frozen cod
   steaks
Juice of ½ lemon
½ oz. butter
2 oz. Gruyère cheese (can be
   processed cheese)

Salt and pepper
1 teaspoon mixed herbs
1 teaspoon beaten egg
Parsley sprigs to garnish

Wash the steaks, brush with lemon juice and place a knob of
butter on each one.

Grill for 6 minutes on one side, then turn and grill for 3 minutes.
While fish is cooking, prepare the topping: sieve the cheese, add
the mixed herbs and bind with beaten egg.
Season.
Spread fish with the prepared cheese topping and grill for a
further 3 minutes.
Serve hot, with grilled tomatoes and creamed potatoes.
Garnish with parsley.

CORNED BEEF AND POTATO PIE

Preparation Time: 15 minutes · Cooking Time: 20-30 minutes

2 onions	Salt and pepper
3 oz. butter	1 teaspoon dried sage
4 tomatoes	5-6 serving packet instant
1 clove garlic	mashed potato
12 oz. can corned beef	

Peel and chop the onions. Sauté in 2 oz. butter until transparent.
Peel and chop the tomatoes. Crush the peeled garlic with a little
salt.
Cut the corned beef into large dice and add to pan with the
tomatoes and garlic. Season well. Transfer to a casserole and
sprinkle with sage.
Make up the mashed potato according to packet instructions,
adding seasoning to taste and the remaining butter. Pile onto
meat mixture and spread across top, forking up the surface.
Glaze with a little milk.
Bake in a moderately hot oven, gas mark 6, 400° F., for 20-30
minutes until golden brown.

CORNED BEEF CASSEROLE

Preparation Time: 15 minutes · Cooking Time: 20 minutes

1 onion	16 oz. can baked beans
2 oz. butter	Salt and pepper
19 oz. can new potatoes	Chopped parsley
12 oz. can corned beef	

Peel and chop the onion. Fry in the butter until soft, but do not
allow it to colour.

Drain the potatoes and cut into slices. Add to the onion and
sauté for about 5 minutes.

Remove half this mixture from the pan, drain on kitchen paper
and reserve for the topping.

Cut the corned beef into cubes and add it with the baked beans
to onion and potatoes in the pan. Season and mix well. Place
in 2-pint casserole and top with the reserved potatoes.

Bake in a moderate oven, gas mark 5, 375° F., for 20 minutes.

Sprinkle with chopped parsley and serve hot.

COTTAGE CHEESE AND SALMON PIE

Preparation Time: 15 minutes · Cooking Time: 20-25 minutes

Two 8 oz. cartons cottage cheese	7½ oz. can red salmon
2 tablespoons tomato purée	7½ oz. packet frozen but thawed puff pastry
1 egg	Beaten egg to glaze
Salt and pepper	

Mix cottage cheese with tomato purée, the egg (beaten) and
salt and pepper.

Drain and flake the salmon, removing any skin and bones. Add
to cheese mixture

Transfer to a pie dish.

Roll out the thawed pastry on a light-floured board to a rectangle slightly larger than the pie dish.

Cut thin strips from the edges and place round rim of pie dish.
Brush with water. Top with pastry lid. Seal well; knock up
edges and 'flute'.

Brush lightly with beaten egg.

Bake in a hot oven, gas mark 7, 425° F., for 20-25 minutes or
until golden-brown. Serve hot.

CREAMED KIDNEYS

Preparation Time: 15 minutes · Cooking Time: NIL

1 onion
½ oz. butter
12 oz. can braised pork kidneys
   in gravy
2 tablespoons red wine

1 teaspoon Worcestershire
   sauce
Salt and pepper
7½ oz. can button mushrooms
2½ fl. oz. soured cream

Peel and chop onion. Sauté it in butter until transparent.
Add the kidneys, wine, Worcestershire sauce and drained mushrooms.
Bring to the boil and simmer for a few minutes.
Stir a little of the sauce into the soured cream and return to saucepan, stirring well.
Bring back to simmering point, continuing to stir; season.
Serve with boiled rice.

DEVILLED MACARONI CHEESE

Preparation Time: 15 minutes · Cooking Time: 20-30 minutes

3 oz. macaroni
½ pint packet cheese sauce
   mix
½ pint milk

1 oz. grated cheese
Salt and pepper
2 tablespoons mild mustard
   pickle

Cook macaroni in boiling salted water as directed on the packet; drain.
Make up cheese sauce as directed on the packet, using the milk.
Stir the cooked macaroni into the sauce, add the pickle, and season to taste.
Turn into an ovenproof dish and sprinkle with cheese.
Bake in a moderate oven, gas mark 4, 350° F., for 20-30 minutes until top is golden brown.
Serves 2-3.

DEVILLED TUNA

Preparation Time: 15 minutes · Cooking Time: 25-30 minutes

2 onions	Tabasco sauce to taste
2 oz. butter	Salt and pepper
1 oz. flour	Two 7 oz. cans tuna
¾ pint milk	2 hardboiled eggs
1 dessertspoon Worcestershire	Brown breadcrumbs
sauce	

Peel and chop the onions.

Melt 1½ oz. butter in a saucepan and sauté the onions until transparent. Stir in the flour off the heat. Return to heat and cook the mixture ('roux') for 2-3 minutes.

Gradually blend in the milk and cook, stirring, until sauce boils and thickens. Simmer for 3 minutes.

Stir in Worcestershire sauce and tabasco and seasoning to taste.

Drain and flake the tuna and arrange in the base of an oven-proof dish.

Remove shells from hardboiled eggs and chop. Sprinkle over the tuna.

Spoon the sauce onto the tuna and egg, top with breadcrumbs and dot with remaining butter.

Bake in a moderate oven, gas mark 4, 350° F., for 25-30 minutes.

FARMHOUSE HAM SUPPER

Preparation Time: 15 minutes · Cooking Time: 15 minutes

9 oz. packet frozen broccoli	4 tablespoons milk
4 slices ham	2 oz. grated cheese
10½ oz. can cream of chicken	
soup	

Cook the broccoli in boiling, salted water; drain.

Arrange in the base of a shallow ovenproof dish. Top with ham slices.

Mix together the soup and milk. Pour over the ham.

Sprinkle on the cheese.

Bake in a very hot oven, gas mark 8, 450° F., for 15 minutes until heated through.

FLORENTINE EGGS

Preparation Time: 15 minutes · Cooking Time: 25-30 minutes

8 oz. packet frozen leaf spinach
Salt and pepper
4 eggs
Nutmeg
½ pint packet cheese sauce mix

½ pint milk
1 tablespoon fresh bread-crumbs
½ oz. butter
Paprika

Cook the spinach in a little boiling salted water; drain. Season with salt, pepper and a little grated nutmeg. Spread across base of a buttered fireproof dish.

Make 4 depressions in the spinach and break an egg into each.

Make up the cheese sauce with the milk, following directions on the packet. Spoon it over eggs and spinach. Sprinkle with breadcrumbs and dot with butter.

Bake at gas mark 4, 350° F., for 25-30 minutes or until eggs are set.

Garnish with a sprinkle of paprika before serving.

(Spinach can be replaced with frozen broccoli spears but the dish will need a new name since 'Florentine' refers only to one using spinach.)

FLORENTINE PANCAKES

Preparation Time: 15 minutes · Cooking Time: NIL

3½ oz. packet batter mix
8 oz. packet frozen leaf spinach
Salt and pepper
4 oz. ham

Little grated nutmeg
½ pint packet mushroom sauce mix
½ pint milk
Oil for frying

Make up the batter, using water, as directed on the packet.

Cook the spinach in a little boiling, salted water, following instructions. Drain.

Add ham, cut into strips. Add salt, pepper and grated nutmeg to taste. Keep warm.

Make up the mushroom sauce as directed on the packet, using the milk.

Heat a little oil in a frying-pan and make the pancakes in the usual way, turning once. Keep them hot on a plate over a pan of hot water.

Place 2 tablespoons of the savoury filling on each pancake and roll up.

Place on a hot serving dish and spoon the mushroom sauce over them.

Serve immediately.

FRANKFURTER QUIBABS

Preparation Time: 15 minutes · Cooking Time: NIL

4 thick German frankfurters ¼ lb. mushrooms
½ lb. small tomatoes (halved) ¼ lb. black pitted olives
1 large green pepper (diced)

Slice the frankfurters into sections. Impale all ingredients on skewers in whatever order you like.

Brush with a little oil and grill for a few minutes.

Serves 6.

GAMMON WITH MUSTARD AND APRICOT SAUCE

Preparation Time: 15 minutes · Cooking Time: NIL

4 thick bacon or gammon 1 tablespoon apricot chutney
steaks Salt and pepper
1 dessertspoon mustard
powder

Remove rind from gammon rashers and snip the fat round the edges.

Grill for 5 minutes.

Meanwhile, mix together the mustard powder and apricot chutney. Add enough water to make a thick paste and season to taste.

Turn the gammon rashers and spread each one with some of the prepared sauce.

Continue grilling until meat is cooked.

HADDOCK CASSEROLE

Preparation Time: 15 minutes · Cooking Time: 20-30 minutes

13 oz. packet frozen but thawed haddock fillets	1 tablespoon chopped parsley Salt and pepper
½ lb. tomatoes	4 fl. oz. cider
¼ lb. mushrooms	1½ oz. grated cheese

Skin the thawed fillets and cut into cubes. Arrange in base of an ovenproof dish.

Peel and slice the tomatoes and slice the mushrooms.

Place on top of fish with the chopped parsley and seasoning.

Add the cider. Cover with lid.

Bake in a moderate oven, gas mark 4, 350° F., for 20-30 minutes, or until fish is cooked.

Sprinkle with grated cheese and brown under a hot grill.

HAM AND CHICKEN PASTY

Preparation Time: 15 minutes · Cooking Time: 20-25 minutes

5 oz. can ham and chicken roll	7 oz. packet frozen but thawed puff pastry
2 pineapple rings	Beaten egg
3 oz. packet cream cheese	

Remove meat from can and cut into ¼ inch dice.

Chop the pineapple rings and add to the meat.

Add the cream cheese and mix well.

Roll out the pastry on a lightly floured board to an oblong approximately 6 inches by 12 inches. Place on a dampened baking sheet.

Place the filling down the centre of the pastry in a long roll. Brush one long edge of pastry with beaten egg; fold the other long edge over filling and seal. Turn join underneath. Seal ends using beaten egg.

Brush top with beaten egg.

Using a sharp knife, cut diagonal slashes across the top of the roll at 1-inch intervals.

Bake at gas mark 8, 450° F., for 20-25 minutes or until golden-brown.

Serve cold with a green salad.

HAM AND MUSHROOM SAVOURY
Preparation Time: 15 minutes · Cooking Time: NIL

5 oz. quick-cooking macaroni	4 slices ham
10 oz. can mushroom soup	15½ oz. can carrots

Cook macaroni in boiling, salted water as directed on packet; drain.

Heat the mushroom soup and the carrots in separte saucepans. Drain carrots.

Stir macaroni into the hot soup and spoon into the centre of a warmed serving dish.

Arrange the carrots round the edge.

Roll each slice of ham and place on top of macaroni mixture.

Serve at once.

HAM AND POTATO CHEESE
Preparation Time: 15 minutes · Cooking Time: 20-30 minutes

4 oz. grated cheese	¼ teaspoon dry mustard
Small can evaporated milk	19 oz. can new potatoes
Salt and pepper	4 oz. ham

Combine the grated cheese and evaporated milk in a bowl standing in a saucepan of hot water, and heat gently until cheese is well softened. Add the seasonings and stir until thick.

Drain potatoes and slice thickly.

Arrange the potatoes and diced ham in alternate layers in a greased ovenproof dish.

Spoon over them the prepared cheese sauce and bake in a moderate oven, gas mark 4, 350° F., for 20-30 minutes.

Serve this on its own or with grilled tomatoes.

MACARONI NEAPOLITAN

Preparation Time: 15 minutes · Cooking Time: NIL

8 oz. quick-cooking macaroni	2 teaspoons beef extract
¼ pint single cream	5 oz. grated Cheddar or Lan-
2 standard eggs	cashire cheese
5 oz. can tomato purée	Salt and pepper

Cook the macaroni in boiling, salted water as directed on the packet; drain.

Meanwhile, beat together the cream, eggs, tomato purée and beef extract.

Return the cooked macaroni to the pan and add the cream mixture, 4 oz. cheese and seasoning. Stir over a gentle heat until very hot but do not allow it to boil.

Transfer to a buttered heat-proof dish and sprinkle with remaining cheese. Brown under a hot grill and serve at once.

MEAT AND POTATO CAKES

Preparation Time: 15 minutes · Cooking Time: NIL

5-6 serving packet crispy fry	3 tablespoons any chutney
potato mix	sauce
7 oz. can luncheon meat	Fat or oil for frying

Make up the potato as directed and leave to stand. Divide into 12 even-sized pieces.

Cut meat into 6 slices.

Press each piece of potato into a flat shape a little larger than the meat.

Brush meat with sauce, then enclose it between 2 pieces of potato, pressing well together and fluting the edges.

Mark the surface in a criss-cross design with a knife. Fry in deep or shallow fat until golden-brown.

Drain on absorbent paper and serve immediately.

MEAT DUMPLINGS IN TOMATO SOUP

Preparation Time: 15 minutes · Cooking Time: NIL

15 oz. can minced meat	3 oz. pre-cooked rice
1 small teaspoon chopped onion	1 egg
1 clove garlic, crushed	1 oz. flour
Salt and pepper	15½ oz. can tomato soup
1 teaspoon dried parsley	Squeeze lemon juice

Mix together the mince, opion, garlic, seasoning, parsley and
    half the rice.
Bind the mixture together with the beaten egg.
Form into small pieces with floured hands and roll into balls on
    a floured board.
Heat the tomato soup in a saucepan, then add the meat balls,
    the remaining rice and the lemon juice and simmer for 10
    minutes.
Serves 6.

MEAT PASTIES

Preparation Time: 15 minutes · Cooking Time: 25 minutes

1 dessertspoon Worcestershire sauce	15½ oz. can beef and vegetable pie filling
Salt and pepper	13 oz. packet frozen but thawed shortcrust pastry

Stir Worcestershire sauce into pie filling and add seasoning to
    taste.
Divide pastry into 6 equal portions, form each one into a ball
    and roll them out on a lightly floured board to circles 6 inches
    in diameter.
Place one-sixth of the filling down the centre of each pastry
    circle.
Wet outside rim of pastry and draw edges together, sealing
    firmly at the top of each pasty.
Place on a baking sheet and bake in a moderately hot oven, gas
    mark 6, 400° F., for 25 minutes or until pastry is golden.

MEXICAN PIE

Preparation Time: 15 minutes · Cooking Time: 45 minutes

1 onion	7 oz. can red peppers (sliced)
1 lb. minced beef	3-4 serving packet instant
7½ oz. can spaghetti	mashed potato
14 oz. can tomatoes	

Fry the onion and when golden add the minced beef until browned.

Put in a greased oven dish with a layer of spaghetti, tomatoes and drained peppers.

Make up the potato according to the instructions on the packet and cover the meat and vegetables.

Bake in a moderate oven, gas mark 5, 375° F., for about 45 minutes.

MINCE-A-RONI

Preparation Time: 15 minutes · Cooking Time: 15 minutes

15 oz. can minced steak	½ pint packet cheese sauce mix
1 tablespoon instant onion	½ pint milk
2¼ oz. can tomato purée	1 oz. grated cheese
7½ oz. can grilling mushrooms	Browned breadcrumbs
Salt and pepper	Little butter
8 oz. quick-cooking macaroni	

Combine minced steak, onion, tomato purée, drained mushrooms and seasoning in a saucepan. Heat gently.

Cook the macaroni in boiling, salted water until tender. Drain. Arrange half in the base of a buttered, ovenproof dish. Top with the meat mixture, then cover with remaining macaroni.

Make up the cheese sauce using the milk and following the directions on the packet. Spoon over the macaroni.

Sprinkle with breadcrumbs and grated cheese and dot with butter.

Bake in a moderately hot oven, gas mark 6, 400° F., for 15 minutes or until top is golden.

MINCE COBBLER

Preparation Time: 15 minutes · Cooking Time: 10-15 minutes

1½ oz. butter	Salt and pepper
7½ oz. can mushrooms or ¼ lb. fresh mushrooms	6 oz. packet scone mix
	3 tablespoons milk or water
15½ oz. can minced beef in gravy	1 teaspoon mixed herbs
	Beaten egg or a little extra milk
1 tablespoon tomato purée	
1 teaspoon Worcestershire sauce	

Slice the mushrooms (if using fresh) or drain (if canned).
Sauté gently in the butter for 3-4 minutes. Add the minced beef, tomato purée, Worcestershire sauce and seasoning to taste. Mix thoroughly, remove from heat.
Make up the scone mix, adding the mixed herbs and seasoning, using milk or water, according to directions on packet.
Roll out as directed and cut into circles using a 2-inch cutter. Brush tops with beaten egg or milk.
Transfer mince mixture to an ovenproof dish. Arrange scone rounds in a circle round edge of dish, overlapping them slightly.
Cook in a hot oven, gas mark 8, 450° F., for 10-15 minutes or until scone mixture is golden and cooked through.

MOUSSAKA

Preparation Time: 15 minutes · Cooking Time: 20 minutes

1 packet white sauce mix	2 tablespoons tomato paste
½ pint milk	¼ teaspoon minced garlic
14¾ oz. can aubergines	Salt and pepper
15½ oz. can minced beef	½ oz. grated cheese

Make up white sauce according to directions on the packet, using the milk.
Place half the aubergines in the base of an ovenproof dish.
Combine tomato paste, minced beef, garlic powder. Season.
Place this mixture over aubergines, and top with remaining aubergines.

Spoon over white sauce and top with grated cheese.
Bake in a moderately hot oven, gas mark 6, 400° F., for about 20
   minutes.

PARISH PIE

Preparation Time: 15 minutes · Cooking Time: 25 minutes

16 oz. can ham
2 hardboiled eggs
4 oz. mushrooms
10½ oz. can condensed mushroom soup

1 tablespoon Worcestershire
   sauce
7½ oz. packet frozen but
   thawed shortcrust pastry

Remove excess jelly from ham and cut the meat into ½-inch
   cubes.
Chop, but not finely, the hardboiled eggs and mushrooms.
Combine soup, Worcestershire sauce, diced ham, and the chopped eggs and mushrooms. Mix lightly together. Turn mixture
   into a 2-pint pie dish.
Roll out the thawed pastry on a lightly-floured board and cover
   the pie with pastry in the usual way. Use trimmings to decorate the pie.
Bake in a hot oven, gas mark 7, 425° F., for 25 minutes or until
   pastry is golden-brown.

PASTA WITH SALMON

Preparation Time: 15 minutes · Cooking Time: NIL

6 oz. pasta shells
½ pint packet parsley sauce
   mix

½ pint milk
Salt and pepper
3½ oz. can salmon

Cook the pasta in boiling salted water until tender; drain.
While the shells are cooking, make up the parsley sauce, using
   the milk and following directions on the packet.
Drain the salmon and remove any skin and bones.
Stir the sauce into the pasta and add the flaked fish. Season.
Serve at once.
Serves 3.

PÂTÉ IN PASTRY

Preparation Time: 15 minutes · Cooking Time: 25 minutes

4 oz. mushrooms
1 oz. butter
7½ oz. packet frozen but thawed puff pastry

4 oz. can liver pâté
Pinch salt
Beaten egg
Paprika

Slice the mushrooms thinly and sauté gently in the butter.
Remove from heat and drain on absorbent paper.
Roll out the thawed pastry on a lightly-floured board to a rectangle about 11 inches by 10 inches. Cut in half lengthwise.
Place one piece of pastry on a dampened baking sheet.
Spread with pâté to within ½ inch of the edges. Sprinkle with salt. Top with the mushrooms. Brush edges with water.
Place remaining pastry rectangle on top. Seal edges together carefully.
Beat the egg with a little paprika and brush pastry with this mixture.
Bake in a moderately hot oven, gas mark 6, 400° F., for about 25 minutes or until golden.
Serve hot or cold, cut into slices.

PEPPER PASTA

Preparation Time: 15 minutes · Cooking Time: NIL

8 oz. shell pasta
1 small onion
1 clove garlic
2 sticks celery
½ oz. butter
14 oz. can tomato juice

¼ pint water
½ teaspoon pepper sauce
¼ teaspoon mixed herbs
Salt
6 oz. grated Cheddar cheese

Cook pasta in boiling, salted water until tender; drain.
While pasta is cooking, peel and slice the onion and slice the celery. Sauté in the butter until soft.
Add tomato juice, crushed garlic, water, salt, pepper sauce and herbs. Stir well. Bring to the boil and simmer for about 5 minutes. Stir in the pasta.
Turn into an ovenproof dish. Sprinkle cheese on top and brown under a hot grill.

POTATO AND HAM OMELETTE

Preparation Time: 15 minutes · Cooking Time: NIL

1 oz. butter	1 oz. chopped ham
1 tablespoon chopped onion	2 eggs
2 tablespoons cooked cubed	Salt and pepper
potato	

Melt the butter in an omelette or frying-pan. Add the onion and
sauté until transparent. Add the potato and cook over a good
heat until onion and potato are turning golden.

Stir in the ham.

Beat the eggs with 2 tablespoons water and some seasoning.

Pour egg mixture into the pan and make the omelette in the
usual way, shaking the pan with one hand while drawing the
cooked egg to the centre of the pan with a fork held in the
other hand, allowing the uncooked egg mixture to flow to the
edges.

When omelette is firm and golden underneath and still faintly
runny on top, fold it in half and slide it onto the warmed
plate.

Serve at once.

POTATO QUICHE

Preparation Time: 15 minutes · Cooking Time: 15-20 minutes

2-3 serving packet instant	4 oz. tomatoes
mashed potato	4 oz. grated cheese
1 oz. butter	2 eggs beaten
1 tablespoon flour	¼ pint milk
Pinch of salt and pepper	

Make up potato as directed, adding butter, flour and seasoning.

Press mixture into a pie plate, lining the plate completely.

Slice tomatoes and place over base of flan. Sprinkle with salt
and pepper.

Put cheese on top.

Heat milk and mix with beaten egg. Pour into flan case and
bake at gas mark 6, 400° F., for 15-20 minutes until golden-
brown.

PRAWN AND TOMATO MACARONI

Preparation Time: 15 minutes · Cooking Time: NIL

14 oz. can tomatoes
1 bayleaf
1 dessertspoon instant onion
¼ teaspoon instant garlic
    powder

Salt and pepper
4 oz. frozen but thawed prawns
6-8 oz. macaroni
2 oz. grated Parmesan cheese

Place tomatoes, bayleaf, onion, garlic and seasoning to taste in
    a saucepan. Bring to boil, simmer for 5 minutes.
Add thawed prawns and cook further 5 minutes.
Meanwhile, cook macaroni according to directions on packet in
    boiling salted water until tender.
Drain well and arrange in a serving-dish.
Mix half the cheese into the macaroni. Spoon sauce over it
    sprinkling the remaining cheese over the sauce.

QUICHE DANOISE

Preparation Time: 15 minutes · Cooking Time: 25-30 minutes

7½ oz. packet frozen shortcrust
    pastry
6 oz. can bacon luncheon meat
1 oz. lard or dripping

2 eggs
6 oz. can cream
Salt and pepper

Roll out the thawed pastry on a lightly-floured board and line
    into a 7-inch flan ring.
Cut the luncheon meat into 6 slices.
Heat the fat in a frying pan and fry the meat for 2 minutes on
    both sides. Remove and drain on absorbent paper. Leave to
    cool.
Beat the eggs, stir in the cream and seasoning.
Arrange the slices of meat in the flan case. Pour in the egg and
    cream mixture.
Cook in a moderately hot oven, gas mark 6, 400° F., for 25-30
    minutes or until top is golden and filling is set.
Serve hot or cold.

QUICK CANELLONI

Preparation Time: 15 minutes · Cooking Time: 30 minutes

6 oz. canelloni or giant rigatoni
½ pint packet savoury white
  sauce mix

½ pint milk
10¾ oz. can Bolognese sauce
1 oz. grated Parmesan cheese

Cook the canelloni or giant rigatoni in boiling, salted water
  until tender. Drain.
Meanwhile, make up the white sauce according to instructions
  on packet, using milk.
Place half the pasta in base of a buttered fireproof dish; cover
  with half Bolognese and half white sauce.
Repeat these layers with remaining pasta and sauces, ending
  with white sauce.
Sprinkle Parmesan cheese over it.
Bake in a moderate oven, gas mark 4, 350° F., for 30 minutes.

QUICK CHICKEN CASSEROLE

Preparation Time: 15 minutes · Cooking Time: 20-30 minutes

4 cooked chicken joints
1 large sliced onion

Medium can mulligatawny
  soup
Salt and pepper

Put chicken joints in a casserole.
Sauté onion gently in butter until transparent and soft.
Put on top of chicken. Season.
Add the can of soup.
Heat in a moderate oven, gas mark 5, 375° F., for 20-30 minutes.
Serve with boiled rice.

QUICK CHICKEN DISH

Preparation Time: 15 minutes · Cooking Time: 15 minutes

1 cooked chicken
7½ oz. can button mushrooms
½ oz. butter
1 clove garlic

10 oz. can cream of mushroom
  soup
10 oz. can cream of tomato
  soup
2 tablespoons dry sherry

Skin the chicken, remove the meat from the bones and cut into bite-sized pieces.

Drain the mushrooms.

Melt the butter in a saucepan and lightly fry the mushrooms for a few minutes. Crush the garlic with a little salt and add to the saucepan with the soups, chicken and sherry.

Heat gently, stirring from time to time, for 15 minutes.

Serve garnished with chopped parsley and croutons of fried bread.

QUICK TUNA SALAD

Preparation Time: 15 minutes · Cooking Time: NIL

Two 7 oz. cans tuna steak	1 small green pepper
19 oz. can new potatoes	1 medium onion
3 tablespoons olive oil	1 crushed clove garlic
2-3 tablespoons lemon juice	2 tablespoons chopped parsley
Salt and pepper	

Drain the tuna and divide carefully into separate pieces.

Drain and slice the potatoes.

Combine olive oil, lemon juice, garlic and seasoning in a bowl and beat them with a fork.

Extract 1 tablespoon of this dressing and put it in a separate bowl, adding the chopped parsley to it.

Peel and slice the onion very thinly. Cut the pepper into thin rings. Add to the plain dressing and toss well.

Add tuna and turn it in the mixture.

Toss potatoes in the dressing and parsley. Arrange round edge of serving-dish. Pile tuna mixture into the centre.

QUICK WELSH PANCAKES

Preparation Time: 15 minutes · Cooking Time: NIL

3½ oz. packet batter mix	4-6 oz. grated cheese
Little lard or oil	Pinch mixed herbs
4 slices ham	

Make up batter mix, using water according to directions on packet.

Heat a little lard or oil in a frying-pan. Pour in enough batter to thinly cover base of pan, and cook quickly until underside is golden-brown. Turn. Cover with a slice of ham, a quarter of the grated cheese, and a pinch of mixed herbs.

When underside is cooked, and the cheese slightly melted, roll up pancake and transfer to a warm serving dish.

Keep hot while making 3 more pancakes in the same way.

Serve with grilled tomatoes.

SALMON IN A BLANKET

Preparation Time: 15 minutes · Cooking Time: 25-30 minutes

½ packet white sauce mix
¼ pint milk
¼ cucumber
7¾ oz. can salmon
2 teaspoons chopped fresh parsley or 1 teaspoon dried parsley

1 tablespoon Worcestershire sauce
Salt and pepper
13 oz. packet frozen but thawed puff pastry
Little beaten egg

Make up the white sauce according to directions on packet but using half the contents of the packet and ¼ pint milk.

Peel cucumber, cut in half lengthways and remove the seeds, using a teaspoon. Dice flesh.

Drain the salmon and flake the flesh, removing any skin and bones.

Mix together the salmon, white sauce, cucumber, parsley, Worcestershire sauce and seasoning.

Roll out the thawed pastry on a lightly-floured board to an 11-inch square. Spread the salmon mixture over the pastry, leaving a 1-inch border round the edge. Brush this border with water.

Bring points of pastry towards centre until edges overlap slightly.

Seal edges firmly. Transfer carefully to a baking sheet. Brush with beaten egg to glaze.

Bake in a hot oven, gas mark 7, 425° F., for 25-30 minutes or until pastry is golden-brown and cooked through.

Serve hot or cold.

SAUSAGE AND APPLE PIE

Preparation Time: 15 minutes · Cooking Time: 20-30 minutes

1 lb. pork sausagemeat	10½ oz. can condensed cream
½ lb. cooking apples	of tomato soup
4 oz. spaghetti	2 oz. grated cheese
	Salt and pepper

Fry the sausagemeat to extract most of the fat.
Peel, core and slice the apples.
Arrange half the drained sausagemeat in a fireproof dish.
Cover with half the apples. Season. Repeat with remaining meat
   and apples.
Cook the spaghetti in boiling salted water until tender; drain.
Place the soup in a saucepan and blend with a ¼ can of water.
   Heat gently. Stir in spaghetti.
Arrange this mixture on top of the apples and sausagemeat.
Sprinkle with grated cheese.
Bake in a moderate oven, gas mark 5, 375° F., for 20-30 minutes
   or until heated through.

SAUSAGE AND CHICKEN PATTIES

Preparation Time: 15 minutes · Cooking Time: 12-15 minutes

1 lb. pork sausagemeat	Seasoned flour or milk and
4⅞ oz. can chicken supreme	browned breadcrumbs
	Fat for frying

Divide the sausagemeat into 8 pieces and form each one into a
   circle about 4 inches in diameter, pressing the meat out on a
   lightly-floured board.
Chop the chicken in its sauce and place a teaspoonful on each
   sausage circle. Draw the edges together, turn and flatten each
   piece to about ½-inch thickness.
Coat each patty with flour, or dip in milk and coat with breadcrumbs.
Fry gently in a little hot fat for 12-15 minutes, turning them
   once.
Drain and serve hot.

SAUSAGE AND CORN PIE

Preparation Time: 15 minutes · Cooking Time: NIL

11½ oz. can sweetcorn
½ lb. sausages
3-4 serving packet instant
  mashed potato

½ pint packet of cheese sauce
mix

Heat sweetcorn in a saucepan, while grilling the sausages.
Put the corn, drained, in a greased ovenproof dish and top with
  the sausages.
Make up the mashed potato as directed on the packet and put
  on top.
Make up the cheese sauce as directed on the packet and pour it
  over the potato.
Put under grill until brown.

SAUSAGE MEAT DROPS

Preparation Time: 15 minutes · Cooking Time: NIL

2 standard eggs
½ lb. pork sausagemeat
4 oz. grated Cheddar cheese

4 tablespoons chopped parsley
Little flour
Oil for frying

Beat the eggs and mix with sausagemeat, cheese and parsley.
Mash all together until well mixed.
Use flowered hands to shape into flat rounds.
Fry in a little hot oil for 5 minutes on each side, until golden.
Serve hot.

SAUSAGE SQUARES

Preparation Time: 15 minutes · Cooking Time: 40 minutes

1 onion
1 oz. dripping or lard
8 oz. pork sausagemeat
2 tablespoons tomato ketchup

13 oz. packet frozen but
  thawed shortcrust pastry
Little milk.

Peel and chop the onion and fry gently in the fat until tender.
Add the sausagemeat and tomato ketchup. Mix well and continue to fry lightly for about 5 minutes.

Meanwhile, roll out the thawed pastry on a lightly-floured board to a rectangle 10 inches by 12 inches. Place on a baking sheet.

Spread the sausage mixture over half the pastry, leaving ½ inch clear along the edges. Damp the edges with water and fold the rest of the pastry over the mixture. Seal edges well. Brush top with milk.

Bake in a moderate oven, gas mark 5, 375° F., for 20 minutes; reduce heat to gas mark 4, 350° F., for another 20 minutes.

Cut into squares and serve hot or cold.

SIMPLE SIMON PIE

Preparation Time: 15 minutes · Cooking Time: 1 hour

2 medium onions	2 tablespoons tomato purée
3 courgettes	¼ pint stock or water
3 tablespoons cooking oil	2 eggs
12 oz. can corned beef	¼ pint milk
3 tomatoes	2 oz. grated cheese
Salt and pepper	

Peel and slice the onions. Wash the courgettes and cut into ¼-inch slices.

Heat the oil in a frying pan and cook the onions and courgettes until just tender.

Chop the corned beef into small pieces. Peel and slice the tomatoes.

Put a layer of fried vegetables into a casserole, then a layer of corned beef, and finally a layer of sliced tomatoes.

Season well and repeat this again until all the vegetables and beef have been used up.

Mix tomato purée and water or stock together, pour over the top and cover. Bake in a moderate oven, gas mark 4, 350° F., for 30 minutes.

Meanwhile, beat eggs, add milk, grated cheese and a little salt and pepper. Remove lid, pour this mixture into the casserole and continue to cook, uncovered, for a further 30 minutes.

SPAGHETTI AND VEGETABLE PIE

Preparation Time: 15 minutes · Cooking Time: 30-35 minutes

8 oz. packet frozen mixed
vegetables
8 oz. can spaghetti rings
3 hardboiled eggs

7½ oz. packet frozen but
thawed shortcrust pastry
Salt and pepper

Place half the mixed vegetables in a 2-pint oval pie dish. Cover
with half the can of spaghetti rings. Season. Cut the shelled
eggs in half lengthwise and place in the dish.
Cover with the remaining vegetables and spaghetti, and season.
Roll out the thawed pastry on a lightly-floured board to a
rectangle slightly larger than the pie dish.
Cut strips from the sides to place round edge of pie dish.
Brush with water and cover with pastry, trimming edges and
sealing well. Brush with milk. Make 2 holes in pastry through
which steam can escape.
Bake in a moderately hot oven, gas mark 6, 400° F., for 30-35
minutes.
Serve hot or cold.

SPEEDY SPANISH OMELETTE

Preparation Time: 15 minutes · Cooking Time: NIL

2 oz. butter
4 oz. onion
8 oz. can tomatoes
2 cooked potatoes

4 eggs
Salt and pepper
Garlic salt

Slice onion thinly and sauté in butter in a large frying pan
until clear. Add tomatoes (drained and cut small) and
potatoes (thinly sliced).
Lightly beat the eggs, season with salt, pepper and garlic salt
and pour into pan.
Cook gently, shaking the pan occasionally, until set.

STEAK AND KIDNEY STEW WITH PARSLEY DUMPLINGS

Preparation Time: 15 minutes · Cooking Time: 15 minutes

4 oz. self-raising flour	1 tablespoon chopped parsley
Pinch salt	15 oz. can steak with kidney
2 oz. shredded suet	pie filling
4 tablespoons water	

Sift flour and salt into a bowl. Add suet and parsley. Stir in the water with a round-bladed knife. Knead until smooth.

Divide dough into 8 pieces and roll into balls.

Empty the can of pie filling into a medium-sized saucepan and add half a can of water. Bring to the boil, stirring occasionally. Reduce heat under saucepan until stew is simmering.

Drop the dumplings into the saucepan, cover with the lid and leave to simmer for 15 minutes.

STEAK AND MUSHROOM PIE

Preparation Time: 15 minutes · Cooking Time: 30 minutes

¼ lb. mushrooms	½ lb. packet puff pastry
1½ oz. butter	Beaten egg
Two 15 oz. cans cooked steak in gravy	

Slice the mushrooms and cook in the butter for a few minutes. Add to the cooked steak. Adjust seasoning.

Transfer steak and mushrooms to a pie dish.

Roll out the puff pastry to a rectangle just larger than the pie dish. Cut strips from edges, place round edge of dish, dampen with water.

Place pastry on top and seal edges firmly. Trim. Make holes for steam to escape. Brush with beaten egg. Decorate pie with trimmings.

Bake at gas mark 8, 450° F., for 15 minutes. Reduce heat to gas mark 4, 350° F., and cook for a further 15 minutes or until pastry is golden and cooked through.

STUFFED COURGETTES

Preparation Time: 15 minutes · Cooking Time: 30 minutes

1 lb. courgettes	Little olive oil
7¾ oz. can Spanish rice	Little butter
2 oz. carton potted shrimps	

Blanch courgettes in boiling, salted water for 5 minutes. Drain.

Combine the shrimps and rice and heat gently, stirring with a fork, until the shrimp butter has melted.

Cut tops from courgettes, and cut the rest of the vegetables in half along their length. Using a teaspoon, scoop out flesh so that shells remain.

Chop flesh and mix with rice. Spoon rice filling mixture into prepared courgette cases.

Brush a baking-tin with a little oil.

Arrange courgettes in the tin and dot each one with a little butter.

Bake in a moderate oven, gas mark 4, 350° F., for 30 minutes.

STUFFED PEPPERS

Preparation Time: 15 minutes · Cooking Time: 40 minutes

4 medium green peppers	1 oz. grated Parmesan cheese
Salt and pepper	1 oz. butter
19½ oz. can beef risotto	

Cut a slice from the top of the peppers and scoop out seeds and pith.

Blanch peppers and their lids in boiling water for 5 minutes; drain. Season insides with salt and pepper.

Meanwhile, make up the beef risotto as directed on the can and mix together the rice and sauce.

Divide risotto between the peppers and top with grated cheese; place the lids back in position.

Stand in a heat-proof dish with a little water and the butter.

Bake, uncovered, in a moderate oven, gas mark 4, 350° F., for 40 minutes, basting once during the cooking time.

Serve hot.

STUFFED TROUT
Preparation Time: 15 minutes · Cooking Time: 30 minutes

½ lb. mushrooms	Salt and pepper
1 onion	Two 12 oz. packets frozen but
1-1½ oz. butter	thawed rainbow trout
2 tablespoons chopped parsley	2 lemons

Peel and chop the onion. Chop the mushrooms finely.

Melt the butter in a sauté pan and cook the onions and mush-rooms gently for 5 minutes. Add the chopped parsley and seasoning. Turn onto absorbent kitchen paper to drain.

Divide the stuffing into four and fill the thawed fish with the mixture.

Place on individual pieces of foil and divide the juice of 1 lemon between the 4 fish, pouring it over them.

Seal the foil, place the parcels on a baking tray.

Bake in a moderate oven, gas mark 4, 350° F., for 30 minutes.

Unwrap carefully and arrange on a large dish, garnished with lemon wedges.

SWEET AND SOUR FRANKFURTERS
Preparation Time: 15 minutes · Cooking Time: NIL

7½ oz. packet frankfurters	2 tablespoons chopped green
4 oz. celery	pepper
1 onion	1 tablespoon cornflour
12 oz. can pineapple cubes	1 tablespoon soy sauce
2 tablespoons oil	2 tablespoons vinegar

Cut the frankfurters and celery into 2-inch pieces. Peel and slice the onion. Drain the pineapple, reserving juice.

Heat the oil in a frying-pan. Add the frankfurters and brown lightly. Add onion and celery and sauté for 5 minutes.

Add pineapple and green pepper and leave on a very low heat.

Put cornflour into a basin and blend into it the soy sauce, vinegar and the pineapple juice, made up to ½ pint with water.

Stir gently into the frying-pan and bring to the boil, stirring. Simmer gently for 5 minutes.

Serve over hot fluffy rice.

SWEET BEAN BAKE

Preparation Time: 15 minutes · Cooking Time: 30 minutes

1 medium onion	16 oz. can baked beans
1 oz. butter	2 dessertspoons sultanas
3 mushrooms	4 rashers streaky bacon

Peel and slice the onion. Heat butter in a saucepan and sauté the onion gently until softened.

Slice the mushrooms. Place half the baked beans in a casserole dish.

Sprinkle with half the sultanas, mushrooms and onion.

Cover with remaining baked beans, then another layer of the remaining sultanas, mushrooms and onion.

Remove rinds from bacon rashers and arrange on top.

Bake uncovered at gas mark 5, 375° F., for 30 minutes.

TOMATO, BACON AND EGG PIE

Preparation Time: 15 minutes · Cooking Time: 40 minutes

7½ oz. packet frozen but thawed shortcrust pastry	3 oz. grated Cheddar cheese
2 eggs	¼ teaspoon dry mustard
3 oz. bacon rashers	Small can evaporated milk
3 tomatoes	Parsley

Roll out the thawed pastry on a lightly-floured board and line into a 7-inch flan ring. Prick base well.

Beat the eggs in a basin, add the diced bacon, peeled and chopped tomatoes, grated cheese and the mustard.

Stir in the evaporated milk.

Bake in a moderately hot oven, gas mark 6, 400° F., for about 40 minutes.

Serve hot or cold, garnished with parsley.

TUNA AND MACARONI CRISP

Preparation Time: 15 minutes · Cooking Time: 10 minutes

4 oz. quick-cooking macaroni
1 small onion
1 oz. butter
10 oz. can cream of mushroom
 soup

7 oz. can tuna
2 oz. cooked peas
¼ teaspoon mixed herbs
Salt and pepper
1 oz. potato crisps

Cook the macaroni in boiling salted water for 7 minutes. Drain.
Peel and chop the onion and fry in the butter until soft without
 colouring.
Add the macaroni to the onion and heat through; add the soup,
 drained and flaked tuna, peas and herbs; season well.
Heat ingredients together, stirring constantly. Pour into a hot
 dish, sprinkle with crushed crisps and grill until golden-
 brown.

VEGETABLE AND CHEESE FLAN

Preparation Time: 15 minutes · Cooking Time: 30 minutes

7½ oz. packet frozen shortcrust pastry
8 oz. packet frozen mixed
 vegetables

3 oz. grated cheese
1 large or 2 standard eggs
¼ pint milk
Salt and pepper

Roll out the thawed pastry on a lightly-floured board and line
 into a 7-inch flan ring.
Cook the vegetables in boiling, salted water for 3 minutes.
 Drain.
Place in flan, top with cheese.
Beat together the egg, milk and seasoning and pour over cheese.
Bake in a moderate oven, gas mark 5, 375° F., for 30 minutes
 or until filling is set.

VEGETABLE PIE

Preparation Time: 15 minutes · Cooking Time: 25-30 minutes

13 oz. packet frozen but
thawed puff pastry
8 oz. packet frozen but
thawed mixed vegetables
14 oz. can tomatoes

¼ teaspoon instant garlic
powder
4 oz. grated cheese
Salt and pepper
Beaten egg

Cut the thawed pastry in half. Roll out each half on a lightly-floured board to 2 oblongs, each measuring 10 inches by 9 inches. Place one piece of pastry on a baking sheet.

Combine the thawed mixed vegetables, the drained tomatoes, garlic and the grated cheese, adding seasoning to taste. Spread this mixture evenly over the pastry on the baking sheet, leaving ½ inch all round. Dampen the edges of the pastry.

Cut 3 or 4 diamond shapes out of the remaining pastry oblong. Place it (now with 3 or 4 diamond-shaped holes) in it on top top of pastry and vegetable mixture. Seal and flute the edges.

Brush with beaten egg and bake in a hot oven, gas mark 7, 425° F., for 25-30 minutes or until pastry is crisp and golden. Serve with a tossed green salad.

20 minutes

BACON, CHEESE AND SWEETCORN FLAN

1 onion
1 oz. butter
1 egg
4 fl. oz. evaporated milk
1 teaspoon prepared mustard
Pepper

3 oz. grated Cheddar cheese
7 oz. can sweetcorn
4 oz. streaky bacon
7½ oz. packet frozen but
thawed shortcrust pastry
1 tomato

Peel and chop the onion. Fry it in the butter until soft and transparent.

Grill until just crisp. Cut into small pieces.

Roll out the thawed pastry on a lightly-floured board and line into a 7-inch flan ring.

Beat the egg, evaporated milk, mustard and pepper together until well blended, then stir in 2½ oz. of the grated cheese, the drained sweetcorn, and the bacon and onion.

Spoon this mixture into the pastry case and spread evenly. Sprinkle with remaining cheese.

Slice the tomato thinly and arrange the slices in a line across the flan.

Bake in a moderately hot oven, gas mark 5, 375° F., for 35-40 minutes until golden-brown.

Serve hot or cold.

BALINESE PORK

Preparation Time: 20 minutes · Cooking Time: 20 minutes

2 pork fillets	9 oz. can risotto
Medium-sized onion	Red pepper (or pepper flakes)
1 tablespoon apple flakes	

Beat fillets flat and cut into strips.

Peel and chop onion.

Fry meat and onions until golden-brown.

Add apple flakes and ¼ pint hot water.

Season, then add the thinly-sliced pepper or pepper flakes and cook gently in a covered pan for 20 minutes.

Serve with risotto (prepared according to instructions on can).

BARBECUED GAMMON

Preparation Time: 20 minutes · Cooking Time: NIL

Gammon steaks	2 tablespoons made mustard
Butter	1 tablespoon vinegar
1 oz. brown sugar	2 tablespoons pineapple juice

Trim gammon steaks and slit the fat. Cook over the fire or barbecue, brushing frequently with butter, for about 10 minutes on each side.

Blend the remaining ingredients and simmer them for 5 minutes.

Serve this sauce with the ham.

BEEF LOAF MOUSSE

Preparation Time: 20 minutes · Cooking Time: NIL

12 oz. can minced beef loaf
4 bunches watercress
1 pint mayonnaise
2 tablespoons French mustard
2 tablespoons sweet brown
  pickle

4 tablespoons double cream
Salt and pepper
1½ oz. gelatine dissolved in 4
  tablespoons hot water
4 egg whites

Pass beef loaf and watercress through a fine mincer, keeping a
  few sprigs of watercress for garnish.
Mix in mayonnaise, mustard, pickle and cream.
Season. Stir melted gelatine into mixture.
Beat egg whites until stiff and fold into mousse.
Pour into a circular mould and chill until set.
Turn out and serve garnished with watercress.

CHEESE AND POTATO CAKES

Preparation Time: 20 minutes · Cooking Time: NIL

5-6 serving packet instant
  mashed potato
Nut of butter
1 oz. flour

2 oz. grated cheese
Salt and pepper
Cayenne pepper
Oil or lard for frying

Make up the potato as directed on the packet, using water and
  a nut of butter.
Stir in the flour and grated cheese. Season with salt, pepper
  and cayenne.
Turn onto a floured board and divide the mixture into 8.
Shape each portion into rounds ½-inch thick, using floured
  hands.
Brown on both sides in hot oil or lard in a frying pan.
Serve hot.

CHICKEN AND HAM CROQUETTES

Preparation Time: 20 minutes · Cooking Time: NIL

5-6 serving packet instant
  mashed potato
½ oz. butter
2 oz. cooked chicken
2 oz. cooked ham
1 teaspoon chopped parsley

Salt and pepper
Nutmeg
I dessertspoon tomato ketchup
Beaten egg
Browned breadcrumbs
Oil for frying

Make up the potato in a large saucepan as directed.
Add the butter, chopped chicken and ham, parsley, seasonings
  and the tomato ketchup. Set the mixture aside to cool slightly,
  then turn onto a floured board and form into oblong shapes.
Brush the croquettes with beaten egg and roll in breadcrumbs.
Fry in hot deep oil for approximately 5 minutes.
Drain on absorbent paper and serve hot, accompanied by
  grilled tomatoes.

CHICKEN LOAF

Preparation Time: 20 minutes · Cooking Time: 30 minutes

10 oz. cooked chicken
8 oz. streaky bacon
½ pint packet bread sauce mix
2 eggs

½ chicken stock cube
¼ pint boiling water
Salt and pepper

Remove chicken flesh from bone and mince with 4 oz. of the
  bacon (rind removed).
Mix with the contents of the packet of bread sauce.
Beat the eggs lightly and dissolve the ½ stock cube in the boiling
  water.
Bind the dry ingredients together with the eggs and stock
  and season with salt and pepper. Using the back of a knife,
  flatten the remaining (de-rinded) bacon and use to line a 1-lb.
  loaf tin. Carefully press the chicken mixture into the tin and
  cover with foil.
Bake in a hot oven, gas mark 6, 400° F., for 30 minutes, removing the foil after 20 minutes.
Turn out and cool.

CHICKEN PANCAKE STACK
Preparation Time: 20 minutes · Cooking Time: NIL

6 oz. packet batter mix
10 oz. can minced chicken pie
    filling

10½ oz. can cut asparagus
    spears
Oil for frying
1 oz. grated cheese

Make up batter using water according to instructions on packet.
Place pie filling and asparagus in separate saucepans and heat
    gently.
Heat a little oil in a frying-pan and pour in enough batter to
    coat surface thinly. Cook until underside is golden, then turn
    the pancake and cook second side.
Remove from pan, repeat with remaining batter.
Stand a heat-proof plate over a pan of boiling water. Place first
    pancake on the plate, cover with half the heated pie filling.
    Place second pancake on top, arrange half the drained aspara-
    gus on pancake and cover with third pancake.
Continue these layers with remaining mixtures, ending with
    a pancake.
Sprinkle grated cheese over top and melt under a hot grill.
Serve cut into wedges.

CURRIED CRAB BOUCHÉS
Preparation Time: 20 minutes · Cooking Time: NIL

12 uncooked frozen but thawed
    vol-au-vent cases
Beaten egg or milk to glaze
Packet curry sauce mix
½ pint milk

3¼ oz. can crab
Salt and pepper
2-3 tablespoons cream
1 teaspoon lemon juice

Glaze and cook the thawed vol-au-vent cases according to
    directions on packet.
Meanwhile, make up curry sauce using milk and following
    packet instructions. Stir in drained and flaked crabmeat.
Season with salt and pepper. Stir in lemon juice and cream.
Remove any uncooked pastry from the centre of the vol-au-vent
    cases and spoon in hot crab filling; top with caps.
Serves 6.

DEVILLED TURKEY LEGS

Preparation Time: 20 minutes · Cooking Time: 45 minutes

2 cold cooked turkey legs	2 tablespoons chutney
2 oz. butter	1 dessertspoon lemon juice
1 onion	1 tablespoon French mustard
1 dessertspoon curry powder	Salt and pepper
1 dessertspoon Worcestershire sauce	

Cut turkey skin from bones and remove skin and sinews. Cut into strips.

Peel and chop the onion and sauté in the butter until transparent.

Stir in the curry powder and cook for a minute or two. Add the remaining ingredients, except the turkey pieces, and simmer for 2-3 minutes.

Add the turkey to the sauce and stir until well coated.

Transfer to an oven-proof dish, cover with the lid, and cook in a moderate oven, gas mark 4, 350° F., for 45 minutes.

Serve with boiled rice or mashed potato.

EGG AND BROCCOLI CHEESE

Preparation Time: 20 minutes · Cooking Time: NIL

9 oz. packet frozen broccoli spears	2 oz. grated Cheddar cheese
2 oz. butter	Salt and pepper
2 oz. flour	Little grated nutmeg
Small can evaporated milk	4 hardboiled eggs

Cook the broccoli in boiling salted water, following directions on the packet; drain. Arrange in the base of an oven-proof dish. Keep warm.

While broccoli is cooking, prepare the cheese sauce.

Melt the butter in a saucepan, stir in the flour and cook the mixture for 2-3 minutes, stirring. Remove from heat and blend in the evaporated milk made up to 1 pint with water.

Return to heat and stir until mixture boils and thickens. Simmer for 3 minutes.

Stir in 1 oz. cheese off the heat. Season with salt, pepper and a little grated nutmeg.

Remove shells from hardboiled eggs and cut into quarters. Arrange on top of broccoli. Spoon the sauce over the top and sprinkle with the remaining grated cheese. Brown under a hot grill.

EGGS IN FISH JACKETS

Preparation Time: 20 minutes · Cooking Time: NIL

7½ oz. packet buttered smoked
  haddock
5-6 serving packet crispy fry
  potato mix

6 hardboiled eggs
Salt and pepper
Oil for deep frying

Cook the haddock following direction on the packet. Remove fish from bag and flake flesh, taking off the skin. Make up the potato as directed on the packet and leave to stand.

Remove shells from hardboiled eggs.

Mix together the fish and potato and add seasoning to taste. Divide the mixture into 6 equal portions. Mould the mixture around the eggs and fry in hot, deep oil until golden brown. Drain.

Serve hot or cold with tomato sauce.

ENTRECÔTE MARCHAND DE VIN

Preparation Time: 20 minutes · Cooking Time: NIL

2 onions
3 oz. butter
1 tablespoon plain flour
4-5 fl. oz. red wine

Juice ½ lemon
1 tablespoon chopped parsley
Salt and pepper
2 lb. entrecôte or rump steak

Peel and chop the onions.

Melt half the butter in a sauté pan and cook the onions until transparent.

Remove pan from heat and stir in the flour.

Return and cook, stirring, for 2-3 minutes. Add the wine, bring to the boil, stirring.

Reduce heat and simmer for a few minutes.

Stir in lemon juice and parsley, then seasoning to taste.
Meanwhile, in a separate pan, melt the remaining butter and
  fry the steak on both sides until cooked to taste, seasoning
  when the meat is sealed.
Transfer to a serving dish and spoon the hot sauce over it.
Serve immediately.

ESCALOPE OF VEAL WITH ARTICHOKES

Preparation Time: 20 minutes · Cooking Time: NIL

4 veal escalopes	3 fl. oz. dry white wine
2 oz. butter	Salt and pepper
6½ oz. can artichoke hearts	1 dessertspoon lemon juice

Using a wooden rolling pin, beat the escalopes on a wooden
  board until quite thin and flat. Trim off any fat.
Melt the butter in a sauté pan.
Add the veal and cook fairly quickly, turning once.
Season.
Drain the artichoke hearts and cut each one in half.
Add them to the pan and heat through.
Pour in the wine and let it bubble for a minute or two.
Adjust seasoning and add lemon juice.
Arrange escalopes on a serving dish.
Place artichokes round them and spoon the sauce on top.

FISH PIES

Preparation Time: 20 minutes · Cooking Time: 30-35 minutes

1½ oz. butter	7½ oz. packet frozen but
1 small onion	thawed puff pastry
4 oz. mushrooms	14 oz. packet frozen but thawed
Salt and pepper	cod steaks
1 dessertspoon chopped parsley	Beaten egg

Peel and chop the onion. Sauté in the butter until transparent.
Chop the mushrooms and add to pan. Cook gently for a few
  minutes; add chopped parsley and seasoning. Put mixture
  on one side to cool.
Roll out the thawed pastry on a lightly-floured board to a

rectangle about 15 inches by 12½ inches. Cut into 4 equal pieces.

Place a thawed cod steak in the centre of each piece of pastry.

Place a quarter of the mushroom mixture on each steak.

Fold the pastry over, sealing the ends and edges with a little water to completely enclose the fish.

Place, sealed edges downwards, in a roasting tin. Brush with beaten egg and make 2 small slits in the top of each puff.

Bake in a hot oven, gas mark 7, 425° F., for 30-35 minutes or until pastry is golden and fish cooked.

Serve hot.

FISH ROLY-POLY

Preparation Time: 20 minutes · Cooking Time: 12-15 minutes

7½ oz. packet buttered smoked haddock	½ pint packet parsley sauce mix
3 large eggs	2 heaped tablespoons instant milk powder
Salt and pepper	1 hardboiled egg

Cook the smoked haddock according to directions on packet.

Remove from bag and pour off the butter. Remove skin from fish and flake flesh.

Grease a Swiss-roll tin measuring about 14 inches by 10 inches then line with a double layer of greaseproof paper. Grease the paper lining also.

Separate the eggs. Stir the yolks into the flaked fish with salt and pepper to taste.

Beat the white stiffly and fold into the fish mixture. Transfer to the prepared tin and spread the mixture out lightly and evenly.

Bake in a moderately hot oven, gas mark 6, 400° F., for 12-15 minutes or until pale brown and springy to the touch.

While fish is in oven, make up the milk using the powder and ½ pint water. Stir into the sauce mix in a pan and cook sauce following directions on packet.

Remove shell from hardboiled egg, chop and stir into sauce.

Turn the roll onto a large piece of greaseproof paper. Carefully loosen the edges and, with the back of a knife, ease the paper away from the mixture. Spread the sauce over the surface, then, using the paper to help, form into a roll. Serve immediately on a warm dish.

FLAMENCO EGGS

Preparation Time: 20 minutes · Cooking Time: NIL

2-3 slices ham	¼ lb. salami
1 small onion	10½ oz. can asparagus tips
Olive oil or butter for frying	Few pieces canned pimento
8 oz. can tomatoes	4-8 eggs
10 oz. can garden peas, drained	Salt and pepper
10 oz. can new potatoes, drained	

Cut the ham into small pieces and peel and chop the onion.
Heat the oil or butter in a sauté pan and cook the ham and onion for a few minutes. Add the tomatoes, peas and potatoes (sliced).
Cook for 3-4 minutes, stirring occasionally.
Add the salami, sliced and cut into strips, and season.
Transfer to an oven-proof dish.
Arrange drained asparagus and pimento, cut into strips, on top.
Break the eggs into the dish and bake in a hot oven, gas mark 7, 425° F., for 5-7 minutes, or until eggs are cooked to taste.

FUNEN PIE

Preparation Time: 20 minutes · Cooking Time: 30-35 minutes

7½ oz. packet shortcrust pastry	½ pint milk
½ lb. onions	Pinch mustard
3½ oz. butter	4 oz. Danish Blue cheese
Salt and pepper	Watercress
1½ oz. flour	

Roll the thawed pastry on a lightly-floured board and line into a 7-8 inch flan ring. Roll out the trimmings and cut into strips to use later for decoration.
Peel and slice the onions. Melt 2 oz. of butter in a saucepan and fry the onions until transparent.

Add the remaining butter to the pan, stir in the flour off the heat and cook the mixture for 2 minutes.

Gradually blend in the milk and stir over heat until mixture becomes very stiff and boils. Simmer for 2-3 minutes.

Mix in mustard, the crumbled or grated cheese and seasoning to taste.

Spoon this mixture into the prepared flan case and arrange the pastry strips in a lattice on top.

Bake in a moderately hot oven, gas mark 7, 425° F., for 15 minutes. Reduce heat to gas mark 4, 350° F., for a further 15-20 minutes, until pastry is cooked. Serve hot or warm decorated with watercress and a tomato salad.

JANSEN'S TEMPTATIONS

Preparation Time: 20 minutes · Cooking Time: 1 hour 30 minutes

4 oz. butter	2 oz. can anchovy fillets, drained
2 medium-sized onions, thinly sliced	2 thinly-sliced pickled herring fillets
2 lb. potatoes, peeled and thinly sliced	Salt and pepper
	¼ pint single cream

Melt 2 oz. butter in a frying-pan and fry onions lightly.

Grease a 2-pint oven-proof dish with 1 oz. remaining butter.

Layer the potatoes, onions, herrings and anchovies in the dish, ending with potatoes. Season.

Dot the surface with the remaining 1 oz. butter.

Cover.

Bake in a moderately hot oven, gas mark 5, 375° F., for 1½ hours or until potatoes are cooked.

Remove from oven. Pour the cream on top.

Serve.

JELLIED MEAT LOAF

Preparation Time: 20 minutes · Cooking Time: NIL

Cup minced ham
2 cups minced cooked veal,
  chicken or turkey
¾ oz. gelatine
2 beef bouillon cubes

1 pint hot water
1 tablespoon lemon juice
½ teaspoon salt
½ teaspoon paprika
3 hardboiled eggs

Mince the meat separately.
Dissolve the gelatine and bouillon cubes in the hot water.
Add lemon juice and salt. Allow to get cold.
Mix the paprika into the minced ham and spread in the bottom
  of a greased 1 lb. loaf tin.
Arrange the shelled eggs lengthwise along the centre.
Spread the minced chicken on top, without packing.
Pour the gelatine mixture over and place the loaf in the re-
  frigerator to chill.
Turn out and serve with tomatoes and watercress and garlic
  bread.
Serves 4-5.

KIPPER KEDGEREE

Preparation Time: 20 minutes · Cooking Time: NIL

5 oz. packet buttered kipper
  fillets
6 oz. quick cooking rice
2 oz. butter

2 hardboiled eggs
1 dessertspoon chopped parsley
Salt and Cayenne pepper
Paprika pepper

Cook the kipper fillets and the rice according to the directions
  on their packets.
Take kipper fillets from the bag and remove skin: flake fish
  roughly.
Melt the butter in a pan, add the rice, shelled and chopped
  hardboiled eggs, chopped parsley and fish, and mix well with
  a fork.
Season to taste with salt and cayenne pepper and warm through
  gently.
Garnish with paprika pepper and tomato wedges.

LEEK AND MUSHROOM SAVOURY

Preparation Time: 20 minutes · Cooking Time: 30 minutes

5-6 serving packet instant mashed potato	10 oz. can cream of mushroom soup
2 oz. butter	Salt and pepper
1 egg yolk	4 oz. Cheddar cheese
Little milk	1 tablespoon breadcrumbs
2 leeks	1 tomato
1 oz. flour	

Make up the potato following the directions on the packet, but adding ½ oz. butter and the egg yolk. Season and leave to cool.

Wash the leeks very well. Trim, and slice.

Melt the remaining butter in a saucepan and sauté the leeks gently. Stir in the flour and cook for a short time. Remove from heat and blend in the soup. Return and stir over heat until sauce thickens and boils.

Grate the cheese and stir all but a tablespoon into the sauce, adding seasoning to taste.

Pipe or fork the potato round the edge of a shallow ovenproof dish, to form a border. Spoon the sauce mixture into the centre.

Mix the breadcrumbs with the remaining cheese and sprinkle over the mushroom mixture. Brush the potato with milk and decorate with the tomato. Cut into slices.

Bake in a moderately hot oven, gas mark 6, 400° F., for 30 minutes, or place under a hot grill until golden brown.

Serve hot.

LUNCHEON MEAT HASH

Preparation Time: 20 minutes · Cooking Time: NIL

2 eggs	12 oz. can pork luncheon meat
19 oz. can new potatoes	Parsley sprigs
1 oz. lard	

Boil the eggs for 10 minutes. Shell and halve lengthwise.

Drain potatoes and dice.

Heat lard in a large frying-pan, add potatoes and sauté for 5
   minutes; add the meat, cubed.
Fry, turning occasionally, till potatoes and meat are browned.
Transfer to a heated serving-dish and garnish with hard-boiled
   eggs and parsley.

MACARONI HOT POT

Preparation Time: 20 minutes · Cooking Time: NIL

6 oz. macaroni	5 oz. can ham and chicken roll
Two ½ pint packets mushroom	Celery salt
sauce mix	2 oz. grated Cheddar cheese
¾ pint milk	3-4 tomatoes
1 small green pepper	Pepper

Cook the macaroni in boiling, salted water for 10 minutes, or
   until tender. Drain.
Make up the mushroom sauce mix according to instructions on
   the packet but using ¾ pint milk.
Cut the ham and chicken roll into ¼-inch dice.
Add cooked macaroni to the sauce, then stir in the seasonings,
   chopped green pepper and meat.
Turn into a shallow ovenproof dish.
Sprinkle with cheese and arrange a row of tomato slices, slightly
   overlapping, at each side of the dish.
Place under a hot grill until golden.

MACKEREL IN WHITE WINE

Preparation Time: 20 minutes · Cooking Time: 20 minutes

1 onion	Strip lemon peel
3 carrots	¼ pint water
1-2 sticks celery	½ pint dry white wine
Bouquet garni	4 small mackerel
6 black or white peppercorns	Salt

Peel and slice onion and carrots. Slice celery.
Put in saucepan with bouquet garni, peppercorns, lemon peel,
   water and wine. Bring to the boil and simmer, covered, for
   10 minutes.

Arrange the cleaned mackerel in an ovenproof dish; sprinkle with salt.

Pour the hot liquid over them.

Cover and cook in a moderate oven, gas mark 5, 375° F., for 20 minutes.

Remove bouquet garni and lemon peel and leave fish to cool in the liquid.

Serve cold, in the liquid, garnished with lemon slices.

MUSHROOM AND SPINACH SAVOURY

Preparation Time: 20 minutes · Cooking Time: 20-25 minutes

2 oz. butter	6 oz. packet frozen chopped
¼ lb. mushrooms	spinach
1 oz. plain flour	Little grated nutmeg
Salt and pepper	1 tablespoon grated Parmesan
¼ pint milk	cheese
	4 eggs

Chop the mushroom and sauté for 2-3 minutes in 1 oz. butter. Stir in the flour and cook this mixture for 2-3 minutes. Then blend in the milk off the heat. Return and stir until mixture boils and thickens. Simmer for 3 minutes. Season. Spoon into a greased ovenproof dish.

Meanwhile, melt remaining butter in a separate saucepan. Add the spinach and cook until thawed. Simmer to evaporate the water. Season with salt, pepper and nutmeg. Add grated Parmesan and the beaten egg yolks.

Beat the egg white stiffly and fold into the spinach mixture. Pour onto the mushroom sauce.

Bake in a moderate oven, gas mark 5, 375° F., for 20-25 minutes or until top is golden and centre has set.

NORMANDY PORK

Preparation Time: 20 minutes · Cooking Time: 50 minutes

1½ lb. pork shoulder cut into	Cup apple sauce
1-inch cubes	2 tablespoons tomato purée
Salt and pepper	½ teaspoon fresh rosemary (or
Cup chopped onion	¼ teaspoon dried)
Clove garlic, crushed	

Remove excess fat from pork and fry gently to extract the dripping.

Remove the brown pieces and brown the pork cubes well on all sides in the dripping. Season with salt and pepper. Place in casserole.

Fry onion and garlic in the fat remaining in the pan until lightly coloured. Stir in apple sauce, tomato purée and rosemary. Season.

Spread all this over the meat in the casserole.

Bake in a moderate oven, gas mark 4, 350° F., for 50 minutes.

Uncover and bake for a further 15-20 minutes.

ORANGE GLAZED HAM

Preparation Time: 20 minutes · Cooking Time: NIL

Large orange	1 oz. raisins
1 oz. soft brown sugar	2 lb. canned ham

Peel rind thinly from half the orange and cut into thin strips; grate off remaining rind. Halve orange and squeeze out juice.

Place orange juice and rinds in a measuring jug and make up to half a pint with water. Place in a saucepan with the sugar and raisins. Bring to the boil, making sure sugar dissolves, and simmer for 12 minutes.

Meanwhile, remove ham from can; wipe off any excess jelly with kitchen paper. Place on a serving-dish.

Pour glaze over ham, arranging the raisins on top.

Make a lattice pattern on sides of meat using the orange strips.

Serve with green salad.

Serves 6-8.

PAELLA

Preparation Time: 20 minutes · Cooking Time: NIL

1 medium onion	7½ oz. can mushrooms
2 tablespoons cooking oil	4½ oz. (drained) can shrimps
¾ pint water	2-3 oz. cooked diced chicken
1 chicken stock cube	2 tablespoons frozen cooked
6 oz. pre-cooked rice	peas
7 oz. can red pimentos	1 bottle mussels

If you haven't a genuine paella dish, a large heavy frying-pan or flame-proof casserole will do just as well.

Skin and slice the onion and cook in the oil until tender but not brown.

Add the water and the stock cube and rice. Bring to boil.

Remove from the heat. Leave to stand for 5 minutes, covered with a lid.

Drain and shred the red pimentos, drain the mushrooms, and drain and rinse the shrimps.

Carefully mix these into the rice with the chicken, peas and the drained mussels.

Heat through very gently and serve piled in a dish.

PASTA WITH HADDOCK SAUCE

Preparation Time: 20 minutes · Cooking Time: NIL

13 oz. packet frozen haddock fillets	15 oz. can mushroom soup
6 oz. pasta shells	3 tomatoes
1 onion	¼ lb. mushrooms
1 clove garlic	2 tablespoons salted peanuts
1 oz. butter	Salt and pepper

Poach the haddock fillets until tender; drain and flake.

Cook the pasta shells in boiling, salted water until tender; drain.

Peel and chop the tomatoes. Peel and chop the onion, slice the mushrooms and crush the garlic with a little salt. Heat the butter in a sauté pan and fry the onion until transparent.

Add the mushrooms and cook for a few minutes. Add the soup and garlic, heat through, then stir in all the other ingredients.

Cook gently for a few minutes then pile into a serving-dish.

PEPPERED FISH STEAKS

Preparation Time: 20 minutes · Cooking Time: NIL

12 oz. packet frozen cod steaks	½ teaspoon pepper sauce
2 oz. butter	1 tomato
1 dessertspoon grated onion	Chopped parsley

Lightly butter grid of grill pan and place fish on it.

Mix butter, onion and pepper sauce together until well mixed. Spread half on top of fish.

Cook for about 8 minutes under grill. Turn fish over and spread with remaining butter. Continue grilling until fish is cooked.

Place a slice of tomato on each steak. Return to grill for a few moments.

Arrange fish on serving dish and pour any melted butter from grill pan over fish.

Serve garnished with parsley.

POLYNESIAN RISOTTO

Preparation Time: 20 minutes · Cooking Time: NIL

1½ oz. butter	7 oz. can sweetcorn kernels
1 small onion	2 oz. pecan nuts or walnuts
5 oz. long grain rice	10 oz. ham
1 chicken stock cube	Canned mango slices, or guava
3 oz. button mushrooms	or apricot halves
Salt and pepper	

Peel and slice the onion. Sauté in the butter until transparent. Add the rice and sauté until opaque.

Dissolve the stock cube in ½ pint boiling water and add to saucepan with the sliced mushrooms and seasoning.

Bring to boil, then reduce heat and simmer very gently, covered, until the rice is just tender and has absorbed all the liquid (about 15 minutes).

Stir in the drained sweetcorn, nuts and diced ham. Return to heat for a few minutes.

Transfer to a heated serving-dish and garnish with drained fruit.

PRAWN AND HADDOCK CASSEROLE

Preparation Time: 20 minutes · Cooking Time: NIL

½ oz. butter	1 teaspoon sugar
1 tablespoon flour	Salt and pepper
14 oz. can tomatoes	1 tablespoon tomato ketchup
1 teaspoon mixed herbs	13 oz. packet frozen but
1 tablespoon instant onion	thawed haddock fillets
1 tablespoon mixed green	4¾ oz. can peeled prawns
peppers	

Melt the butter in a saucepan over a gentle heat, add the flour and cook for a few minutes, stirring constantly. Add the canned tomatoes, herbs, onion, peppers, sugar, seasoning and tomato ketchup. Cover and simmer for 5 minutes.

Skin the fish and cut into 1-inch cubes. Add to the pan and cook for a further 5 minutes, then add the drained and rinsed prawns.

Cook for a further 5 minutes.

Serve with boiled rice.

PRAWN SOUFFLÉ WITH SHERRY SAUCE

Preparation Time: 20 minutes · Cooking Time: NIL

¼ pint white sauce	Salt and pepper
2 eggs, separated	½ oz. butter
1 tablespoon grated cheese	2 egg yolks
2¾ oz. (drained weight) can prawns	1 tablespoon sherry

Blend the white sauce with 2 egg yolks and the cheese.

Mix in the prawns and the seasoning.

Whisk 2 egg whites until really stiff and fold very lightly into the prawn mixture.

Turn into a buttered soufflé dish and bake in the centre of a hot oven, gas mark 6, 400° F., until well risen.

Meanwhile, make the sherry sauce: Whisk 2 egg yolks and the sherry over hot water until light and fluffy.

Serve soufflé with warm sauce.

Serves 2.

PUFF PIZZA

Preparation Time: 20 minutes · Cooking Time: 20 minutes

7½ oz. packet frozen thawed puff pastry	Salt and pepper
	½ teaspoon oregano
1 large onion	6 oz. Gouda cheese
2 oz. unsalted butter	2 oz. can anchovies
8 oz. can tomatoes	Black olives

Roll out the thawed pastry on a lightly-floured board to a rec-

tangle 10 inches by 7 inches. Place on a damp baking sheet.
Peel and chop the onion and sauté in the butter until transparent. Add the tomatoes, seasoning and oregano and cook
for 5-10 minutes or until most of the tomato liquid has evaporated. Spread over the pastry base to within 1 inch of the edge.
Grate the cheese and sprinkle over the tomato mixture.
Arrange a lattice of drained anchovy fillets on top and place a
black olive in the centre of each diamond.
Bake in a hot oven, gas mark 7, 425° F., for about 20 minutes
or until the pastry is well-risen and golden-brown.

QUIBABS

Preparation Time: 20 minutes · Cooking Time: 10 minutes

4 rashers streaky bacon	8 oz. can cocktail sausages
7 oz. can luncheon meat	7½ oz. can grilling mushrooms
12 oz. can pineapple chunks	

Remove rind from bacon rashers and flatten each piece using
the back of a knife; cut each rasher in half crosswise, then
halve each piece lengthwise. Cut the luncheon meat into 16
cubes.
Drain the pineapple, sausages and mushrooms from their liquids.
Reserve 1 tablespoon each of pineapple juice and mushroom
liquor and combine.
Wrap a piece of bacon round each piece of luncheon meat.
Spear the pineapple chunks, sausages, mushrooms and bacon-
wrapped luncheon meat cubes onto 4 long skewers.
Place under a hot grill, and cook for about 10 minutes, turning
once and brushing the quibabs during cooking with the reserved pineapple and mushroom liquor.
Serve with boiled rice.

SALMON, PRAWN AND ANCHOVY FLAN

Preparation Time: 20 minutes · Cooking Time: 25 minutes

7½ oz. packet frozen thawed shortcrust pastry
7¾ oz. can red salmon
1 small onion
¼ pint single cream
2 eggs

2 tablespoons Worcestershire sauce
2 oz. frozen peeled prawns
Salt and pepper
A few green olives
2 oz. can anchovy fillets

Roll out the pastry on a lightly-floured board and line into an 8-inch flan ring. Prick base well. Line with aluminium foil or greaseproof paper and beans or rice and bake 'blind' in a moderately hot oven, gas mark 6, 400° F., for 10 minutes.

Remove foil or paper and beans or rice and bake for a further 5 minutes.

Meanwhile, prepare the filling: drain the salmon, remove skin and bones, and flake flesh. Peel and grate the onion. Reserving a few prawns for decoration, chop the remainder.

Combine flaked salmon, chopped prawns, cream, beaten eggs, grated onion and the Worcestershire sauce. Add seasoning to taste.

Turn into a flan case and bake in a moderate oven, gas mark 4, 350° F., for 25 minutes or until filling has set.

Cool.

Decorate with a lattice of drained anchovy fillets, and arrange stoned halved olives and the reserved whole prawns on top.

SAUSAGE, EGG AND BACON DISH

Preparation Time: 20 minutes · Cooking Time: 30-40 minutes

1 lb. sausagemeat
Garlic powder
½ teaspoon dried parsley
Level teaspoon dry mustard
2 tablespoons flour
4 rashers streaky bacon
4 eggs, beaten

7 oz. can red peppers.
7½ oz. can mushrooms
1 tablespoon Parmesan cheese
2 tablespoons milk
Salt and pepper
¼ teaspoon grated nutmeg
Little butter

Mix meat, garlic, parsley and mustard with a fork.

Line a sandwich tin with the mixture, using the flour to simplify handling.

Cut the bacon into small squares and fry. Drain.

Add mushrooms and bacon to beaten eggs along with drained peppers, cheese, milk, salt and pepper and nutmeg.

Turn into flan case and bake at gas mark 5, 375° F., for 30-40 minutes until filling has set. When cooked, drain off excess fat.

This dish can be cooked in advance and heated through later.

SAUSAGES WITH BANANA AND SWEET CORN FRITTERS

Preparation Time: 20 minutes · Cooking Time: NIL

1 lb. pork sausages	1 large egg
Lard for frying	2 tablespoons milk
4 rashers back bacon	Salt and pepper
7 oz. can sweetcorn	4 firm bananas
2 tablespoons self-raising flour	1 oz. butter

Fry the sausages in lard; drain and keep hot.

To make the corn fritters, mix together chopped, de-rinded bacon, drained sweetcorn, flour, beaten egg, milk and seasoning.

Drop spoonsful of the mixture into hot fat; allow mixture to set and underside to brown before turning, and allow to cook for a further 3-4 minutes.

Drain on absorbent paper. Keep hot.

Peel and slice the bananas. Toss in the melted butter over a gentle heat until softened and golden. Do not overcook since they will break on removal from the pan.

Arrange the sausages, fritters and bananas on a serving dish and serve at once.

SCAMPI PROVENÇALE

Preparation Time: 20 minutes · Cooking Time: NIL

8 oz. long-grain rice	2 tablespoons olive oil
8 oz. frozen thawed scampi	1 clove garlic
1 onion	8 oz. can tomatoes
1 green or red pepper	¼ pint dry white wine
1 oz. butter	Salt and pepper

Cook the rice in boiling, salted water until tender. Drain.

Drain the thawed scampi on absorbent paper.

While the rice is cooking, peel and chop the onion.

Remove seeds and pith from pepper, then chop it.

Heat the butter and oil in a sauté pan and cook the onion and pepper until tender.

Add the strained and chopped tomatoes, the garlic (peeled and crushed with a little salt), and the wine.

Add scampi and continue to cook slowly for a further 5 minutes. Season.

Add the rice to the pan to heat through, mixing it into the sauce with a fork.

Serve very hot.

SMOKED HADDOCK CRUNCH

Preparation Time: 20 minutes · Cooking Time: 15 minutes

7½ oz. packet buttered smoked haddock fillets	2 oz. butter
Salt and pepper	7 oz. can sweetcorn with peppers
Small can evaporated milk	1 oz. grated Cheddar cheese
2 oz. flour	Small packet plain crisps

Cook the smoked haddock according to directions on the packet.

While it is cooking, make up the evaporated milk to 1 pint with water, and whisk in flour.

Place in a saucepan with the butter and stir over a moderate heat until the sauce boils and thickens. Simmer for 2-3 minutes before removing from heat.

Remove the skin from the haddock and flake flesh with a fork.

Stir into the sauce with any liquid from the bag in which it was cooked, and add the drained sweetcorn. Adjust seasoning.

Place in a 2-pint dish. Sprinkle with grated cheese and top with the roughly crushed crisps.

Place in a moderately hot oven, gas mark 6, 400° F., for 15 minutes.

SMOKED HADDOCK OMELETTE

Preparation Time: 20 minutes · Cooking Time: NIL

3 eggs
¼ pint double cream

7½ oz. packet frozen smoked haddock fillets

Cook haddock fillets according to instructions on packet.

Remove skins, flake flesh, dot with butter and keep hot.

Beat eggs, add 1 tablespoon cream and 1 teaspoon water and stir thoroughly.

Grease pan and cook omelette but only until the mixture is beginning to set.

Place fish evenly on top of omelette and put under a hot grill for a few seconds before serving.

SMOKED HADDOCK QUICHE

Preparation Time: 20 minutes · Cooking Time: 30–35 minutes

8 oz. packet buttered smoked haddock
7½ oz. packet frozen thawed shortcrust pastry
¼ pint milk

2 eggs
1 tablespoon chopped parsley
Salt and pepper
2 tomatoes

Cook the haddock according to packet instructions.

Roll out the thawed pastry on a lightly-floured board and line into a 7-inch flan ring.

Reserve the fish liquor from the bag. Skin and flake the fish.

Beat together the milk and eggs; add the parsley, seasoning, fish and fish liquor.

Spoon mixture into the prepared flan case and bake in a moderately hot oven, gas mark 6, 400° F., for 30–35 minutes until filling has set.

Garnish with sliced tomatoes before serving hot or cold.

SWEET AND SOUR CRISPY CODS
Preparation Time: 20 minutes · Cooking Time: NIL

2 7 oz. packets crispy cod fries	¼ pint water
1 onion	2½ oz. sugar
1 small green pepper	Salt
Oil for frying	1 dessertspoon cornflour
⅛ pint white vinegar	

Fry the crispy cods in shallow or deep fat according to directions on packet.

Drain and keep hot.

Meanwhile, peel and slice the onions and slice the green pepper, having removed seeds and pith.

Heat a little oil in a frying pan and cook the vegetables for 2-3 minutes. Add the vinegar, water and sugar and salt to taste. Bring to boil.

Mix the cornflour with a little cold water and add to sweet and sour mixture. Stir until sauce thickens.

Arrange crispy cods in a serving dish. Spoon sauce over them.

Serve with boiled rice.

TUNA IN MUSHROOM AND PEPPER SAUCE
Preparation Time: 20 minutes · Cooking Time: NIL

1 small green pepper	2½ fl. oz. single cream
2½ oz. butter	1 canned red pimento
¼ lb. button mushrooms	7 oz. can tuna steak
1½ oz. flour	Salt and pepper
¼ pint milk	Little lemon juice
8 fl. oz. vegetable stock	

Wash the green pepper and remove seeds and pith. Cut into small dice.

Heat 1 oz. butter in a small pan and sauté the green pepper for 5 minutes. Slice the mushrooms thinly, add to pan and cook for a further 5 minutes.

Meanwhile, melt the remaining butter in another saucepan. Stir in the flour off the heat, return to heat and cook mixture for 2-3 minutes; remove from heat and gradually blend in milk and stock.

Bring to the boil, stirring; reduce heat and simmer for 2-3 minutes. Allow sauce to cool slightly before stirring in cream.

Drain and chop the red pimento. Add to the sauce with the
green pepper and mushrooms.

Drain and flake the tuna, add to sauce and reheat, stirring for 5
minutes. Do not boil. Season with salt, pepper, lemon juice.

Serve hot with rice.

TUNA VOL-AU-VENTS

Preparation Time: 20 minutes · Cooking Time: NIL

12 small frozen vol-au-vent cases	⅓ pint milk
1 packet sauce mix (white, mushroom or onion)	7 oz. can tuna fish

Bake vol-au-vent cases as directed on packet.

Meanwhile, make the sauce using the milk.

Drain tuna, flake roughly and stir into sauce. Fill cases with
the mixture.

TURKEY WITH CHESTNUT AND CRANBERRY BOUCHÉS

Preparation Time: 20 minutes · Cooking Time: NIL

12 frozen vol-au-vent cases	2 tablespoons cornflour
15¼ oz. can turkey with chest-nut and cranberry soup	8 oz. cooked turkey
1½ tablespoons whole berry cranberry sauce	Salt

Glaze and cook the thawed vol-au-vent cases according to directions on packet. Keep warm.

Meanwhile, prepare the filling: chop the turkey meat. Blend a
little of the soup with the cornflour to form a smooth cream.

Warm the remaining soup with the cranberry sauce and pour
onto the blended cornflour, stirring well.

Return to the pan, bring to the boil and boil for 1 minute, stirring constantly.

Add the chopped turkey and salt to taste. Heat through
thoroughly.

Remove lids from cooked vol-au-vent cases and scoop out any uncooked pastry. Spoon in the hot filling and replace the lids. Serve hot.

25 minutes

BANANA-BAKED SOLE

Preparation Time: 25 minutes · Cooking Time: 15 minutes

Butter	Salt
2 fillets lemon sole per person	Freshly-ground pepper
Marjoram	Dry white wine
Small slivers lemon rind	2 bananas

In a large baking tin place a piece of foil at least twice the size of the tin.

Grease the foil lightly with butter. Place the fillets flat on the foil, sprinkle with a little marjoram and dot with lemon rind and small knobs of butter. Season with salt and pepper.

Pour over enough white wine to cover the fish.

Close foil firmly to make it airtight.

Bake at gas mark 4, 350° F., for 15 minutes.

Remove tin. Open 'envelope' and put slices of the bananas, cut lengthwise, between fillets.

Return to oven for a further 15 minutes cooking. Use the juices, unthickened, as a sauce.

CHEESE AND CORN FLANS

Preparation Time: 25 minutes · Cooking Time: 15 minutes

8 oz. plain flour	4 oz. streaky bacon
½ teaspoon salt	4 tomatoes
4 oz. unsalted butter	1 teaspoon prepared mustard
11 oz. Gouda cheese	Salt and pepper
7 oz. can sweetcorn kernels	

Sift the flour into a bowl with the salt. Rub in the butter, then add 3 oz. of the Gouda, finely grated. Mix to a stiff dough using a little cold water.

Roll out the pastry on a lightly-floured board and cut out 8 circles slightly than individual Yorkshire pudding tins, or individual flan cases.

Line the pastry into the tins, prick bases and line with aluminium foil or greaseproof paper, weighted down with rice or dried beans.

Bake pastry cases 'blind' in a moderately hot oven, gas mark 6, 400° F., for 10 minutes. Remove paper or foil and beans or rice and return to oven for a further 5 minutes to dry out.

While pastry is cooking, prepare the filling. Drain the sweetcorn; grill the de-rinded bacon until crisp, then chop; peel and chop the tomatoes; grate the remaining Gouda.

Combine sweetcorn, bacon, tomatoes, cheese, mustard and seasoning. Spoon into prepared pastry cases and return to oven for a further 15 minutes, or until golden-brown.

Serve hot or cold.

CHEESE AND WATERCRESS FLAN

Preparation Time: 25 minutes · Cooking Time: 40 minutes

7½ oz. packet frozen but thawed shortcrust pastry	¼ pint milk
2 eggs	3 oz. processed Gruyère cheese
4 oz. can cream	½ bunch watercress
	Salt and pepper

Roll out thawed pastry on a lightly-floured board and line a 7-inch flan ring with it; prick base with a fork and line flan with aluminium foil. Bake 'blind' at gas mark 5, 375° F., for 10 minutes. Remove foil.

Meanwhile, prepare filling: Beat the eggs in a basin and mix in the cream, milk, sieved cheese, chopped watercress and seasoning.

Pour into the partially-cooked pastry case and return to the oven with the temperature reduced to gas mark 4, 350° F., for 40 minutes or until the filling is set.

Serve cold.

(To 'bake blind' means to cook a flan case without its fillings. The uncooked pastry case is lined with aluminium foil or greaseproof paper, and rice or dried beans can be added for weight.)

CHICKEN IN AN OVERCOAT

Preparation Time: 25 minutes · Cooking Time: 1 hour 45 min.

¾ lb. continental liver sausage
1 tablespoon dry sherry or
   brandy
Little garlic powder
Salt and pepper
¼ lb. button mushrooms

1 oz. butter
Boned stuffed chicken
13 oz. packet frozen but
   thawed puff pastry
Beaten egg

Mash the liver sausage and stir in sherry or brandy, the garlic
   powder and seasoning.
Remove the stalks from the mushrooms and sauté them in the
   butter for 5 minutes, turning them once. Drain on absorbent
   paper.
Remove chicken from its bag. The skin may also be removed
   carefully but this makes the coating more difficult because
   there will be nothing to hold the chicken together.
Place the chicken on a baking sheet and spread the liver sausage
   mixture all over to enclose the chicken entirely. Press the
   mushrooms into the top and sides. Refrigerate.
Roll out the thawed pastry thinly on a lightly-floured board to
   a 12-inch square. Place the chicken, upside down, diagonally
   across the pastry. Damp pastry edges with water and draw
   them towards the centre, sealing them together carefully.
   Cut off and save excess pastry for decoration.
Transfer chicken to a small roasting tin, sealing pastry edges
   under the bird. Brush with beaten egg.
Cut leaves from trimmed pastry and arrange them on top,
   glaze with egg.
Bake in a hot oven, gas mark 7, 425° F., for 15 minutes. Reduce
   heat to moderate, gas mark 4, 350° F., for 1½ hours.
Serve hot or cold, cut into slices

COD STEAK MAYONNAISE

Preparation Time: 25 minutes · Cooking Time: NIL

Large packet frozen cod steaks	1 tablespoon mayonnaise
2-3 serving packet instant mashed potato	Salt and pepper
	Lettuce leaves
2-inch length cucumber	1 tomato
1 hardboiled egg	Extra mayonnaise

Poach the cod steaks in lightly-salted water for 10-15 minutes. Drain and flake coarsely.

While fish is cooking, make up instant mashed potato according to directions on the packet; peel and dice the cucumber.

Shell the hardboiled egg and chop.

Mix together the flaked fish, potato, cucumber, hardboiled egg and mayonnaise and season well.

Press mixture into a well-oiled mould and refrigerate until firm.

To serve: Remove skin from the tomato and cut into quarters, remove seeds, then cut into strips.

Unmould fish onto a bed of lettuce and garnish top with strips of tomato and piped mayonnaise.

EGGOMANIA

Preparation Time: 25 minutes · Cooking Time: 30 minutes

1 large onion	1½ oz. flour
2½ oz. butter	1 teaspoon prepared English mustard
4 hardboiled eggs	
½ lb. tomatoes	Salt and pepper
Small can evaporated milk	6 oz. grated Cheddar cheese

Peel and slice the onion. Fry gently in 1 oz. butter until soft.

Shell and slice hardboiled eggs. Peel and slice tomatoes.

Arrange in layers in a fairly large but shallow ovenproof dish.

Make the evaporated milk up to ¾ pint with water and whisk in the flour and mustard. Place in a saucepan with the onion and remaining butter and stir over a moderate heat until the sauce thickens.

Continue to cook, stirring, for a further 2 minutes. Remove from heat and stir in 4 oz. cheese. Season.

Pour the cheese sauce over the egg and tomato mixture. Sprinkle with the remaining cheese.

Bake in a moderately hot oven, gas mark 6, 400° F., for 30 minutes.

FISH BALLS

Preparation Time: 25 minutes · Cooking Time: NIL

13 oz. packet frozen haddock fillets
Bouquet garni
6 black peppercorns
5 oz. packet instant mashed potato
½ teaspoon fish seasoning

1 tablespoon chopped parsley
Salt and pepper
Seasoned flour
Beaten egg
Browned breadcrumbs
Oil for deep frying

Place the haddock fillets in a shallow pan with the bouquet garni and peppercorns. Barely cover with water, bring to boil and simmer gently for 10-15 minutes or until fish is cooked. Drain. Remove skin and any bone from the fish and flake flesh.

Make up the instant mashed potato following directions on the packet. Cool.

Mix together the flaked fish and mashed potato. Add fish seasoning, chopped parsley and salt and pepper.

Divide mixture into 8. Form each one into a ball. Roll in seasoned flour, dip in beaten egg, then coat with breadcrumbs.

Fry the balls in hot, deep oil until golden. Drain on absorbent paper and serve hot.

Tartare sauce is a good accompaniment to them.

HADDOCK STEAKS FLORENTINE

Preparation Time: 25 minutes · Cooking Time: NIL

13 oz. packet frozen haddock fillets
½ pint milk
12 oz. packet frozen chopped spinach
Packet cheese sauce mix

Salt and pepper
Little grated nutmeg
½ oz. grated cheese
Browned breadcrumbs
Little butter

Poach the haddock steaks gently in the milk for 10-15 minutes, or until cooked. Remove steaks from the pan and keep warm, reserving the liquor.

Cook the spinach according to the packet instructions, season with salt, pepper and a little grated nutmeg.

Place in an ovenproof dish. Arrange fish steaks on top.

Make up the cheese sauce according to directions, using the reserved liquor.

Spoon it over the fish and sprinkle with the grated cheese. Dot with butter and dust with breadcrumbs.

Grill until lightly-browned and serve immediately.

PLAICE WITH GHERKIN SAUCE

Preparation Time: 25 minutes · Cooking Time: NIL

13½ oz. packet frozen plaice
    fillets
¼ pint milk
2 oz. seasoned flour
Browned breadcrumbs
Oil for frying

3 gherkins
2 teaspoons piccalilli
6 tablespoons vinegar
1 small can or ½ large can
    sweetened condensed milk

Begin by making the sauce.

Chop the gherkins and the vegetables in the piccalilli. Stir the vinegar into the condensed milk and add the gherkins and piccalilli. Put in a cool place.

Brush each thawed plaice fillet with the milk and then coat with the flour.

Gently brush the floured fish with the milk again and then turn in the crumbs, ensuring the fish is evenly coated. Press the crumbs into the fish.

Gently fry the fish in shallow, hot oil until golden brown. Drain on absorbent paper.

Arrange fish on serving dish, garnished with lemon slices and parsley sprigs.

Serve the sauce separately.

PORK STEW

Preparation Time: 25 minutes · Cooking Time: NIL

2 onions	½ lb. button mushrooms
2 lb. lean shoulder of pork	A few frozen peas
Garlic	Oil for frying
Large can tomato soup	

Slice onions.

Cut pork into thin strips or small cubes and fry with the onion until tender and turning golden.

Season and add garlic.

Add tomato soup and simmer until the soup begins to reduce and thicken.

Add the mushrooms.

After 2 minutes, pour all this into a dish.

Cook the peas along with those for the vegetable course and sprinkle them over the stew before serving.

Serve immediately.

SAUSAGE AND BACON QUIBABS

Preparation Time: 25 minutes · Cooking Time: NIL

1 lb. pork sausages	1 small or ½ large green pepper
8 rashers streaky bacon	8 bay leaves
4 button onions	Oil
4 button mushrooms	Chopped parsley

Twist each sausage in half and separate.

De-rind the bacon and roll up each rasher.

Skin and parboil the onions for 5 minutes.

Trim the mushrooms. Blanch them by dipping them for 30 seconds into boiling water; this prevents them breaking when you push the quibab skewer through.

Cut the green pepper into chunks.

Thread all the ingredients onto 4 skewers alternately with the bayleaves.

Brush the quibabs with oil.

Grill for 15 minutes on high setting.

Sprinkle with chopped parsley.

Serve with boiled rice or sliced baked potatoes.

SPICED GAMMON

Preparation Time: 25 minutes · Cooking Time: NIL

3 oz. sultanas
2 cloves
15 oz. can crushed pineapple
4 gammon rashers
1 dessertspoon arrowroot or
  cornflour

3 oz. soft brown sugar
Salt and pepper
1 oz. butter
1 dessertspoon lemon juice

Put sultanas and cloves in a saucepan with the syrup strained
   from the can of pineapple and made up to ½ pint with water.
   Bring to boil and simmer for 10 minutes.
Remove the rind from the gammon and snip the fat round the
   edges. This helps to prevent the rashers from curling while
   cooking.
Grill for 5-7 minutes on each side.
Remove cloves from syrup, add sugar, pineapple and seasonings.
   Mix the arrowroot or cornflour with a little cold water and
   add to sauce. Stir well as mixture thickens.
Add butter and lemon juice.
Arrange gammon rashers on a hot serving plate and spoon the
   sauce over them.

SCONE MIX PIZZA

Preparation Time: 25 minutes · Cooking Time: 20-25 minutes

2 onions
1 oz. butter
2 or 3 tomatoes
5 oz. scone mix
Salt and pepper
Pinch mixed herbs

3 tablespoons milk or water
2 processed Cheddar cheese
  slices
Anchovy fillets
Black olives

Peel the onions and slice thinly. Sauté in the butter over a gentle
   heat until transparent.
Peel and slice tomatoes.
In a bowl, combine the scone mix, salt, pepper and herbs. Mix
   to a soft dough with the milk or water.

Transfer to a floured board and knead lightly. Place on a baking sheet and shape into a round 8 inches in diameter by gently pressing out the dough.

Arrange onions and tomato slices on the dough; sprinkle with salt and pepper. Cover with quartered cheese slices and decorate with drained anchovy fillets and black olives.

Bake at gas mark 6, 400° F., near the top of the oven for 20-25 minutes.

Serve hot.

TUNA FISH CAKES

Preparation Time: 25 minutes · Cooking Time: NIL

4 oz. packet frozen garden peas	Dash of Worcestershire sauce
2¾ oz. packet instant mashed potato	Seasoned flour
	Oil for frying
7 oz. can tuna	Salt and pepper

Cook the peas in lightly-salted water until tender; drain.

Make up instant mashed potato as directed on packet.

Drain and flake tuna.

Place the tuna, potatoes and peas in a bowl and mix well together, adding a dash of Worcestershire sauce and seasoning to taste.

Shape mixture into about 12 flat cakes, coat in seasoned flour and fry for 6-8 minutes until golden-brown, turning once.

Serve immediately.

30 minutes

HADDOCK WITH ALMONDS

Preparation Time: 30 minutes · Cooking Time: NIL

2 haddock fillets	1 full teaspoon anchovy essence
½ pint milk	1 oz. flaked almonds
½ pint packet savoury white sauce mix	Pepper

Bake fish in oven in the milk for 20 minutes at gas mark 5, 375° F. If frozen, it will take 10 minutes longer.

When cooked, add the liquor to make up the white sauce mix
   according to directions on the packet.
Mix in the anchovy essence and the pepper (you won't need salt
   because of the anchovy), then the flaked almonds.
Pour over the fish and brown under a hot grill.

Vegetables/Salads/Sauces

Vegetables/Salads/Sauces - 5 minutes

BARBECUE BEANS

Preparation Time: 5 minutes · Cooking Time: 30-40 minutes

16 oz. can baked beans in
tomato sauce
4 tablespoons tomato ketchup
1 tablespoon treacle
2 tablespoons brown sugar

1 tablespoon dried sliced onions
1 tablespoon dried mixed
peppers
A few drops tabasco or chili
sauce

Combine all ingredients in a casserole dish.
Cover and cook in a moderate oven gas mark 4, 350° F., for 30-40 minutes.
Serve with grills or cold meats.

BERNY POTATOES

Preparation Time: 5 minutes · Cooking Time: NIL

Fat or oil for deep frying
2-3 serving packet instant
mashed potato

1 oz. butter
1 egg, beaten
Nibbed almonds

While fat is heating, make up potato as directed and add 1 oz. butter and half the beaten egg.
Form the mixture into balls (walnut size) and coat with the remaining egg, roll in nibbed almonds.
Fry in deep fat or oil.

FIVE-MINUTE MAYONNAISE

Preparation Time: 5 minutes · Cooking Time: NIL

1 small can sweetened condensed milk
¼ pint olive oil
¼ pint vinegar

2 egg yolks
½ teaspoon salt
1 teaspoon French mustard
Dash of Cayenne pepper

Combine all ingredients in a basin and whisk very quickly until well combined (about 1 minute).
Put aside until thick. This takes only a matter of seconds.
Store in airtight jar in a cool place.

MAYONNAISE AND TOMATO DIP
Preparation Time: 5 minutes · Cooking Time: NIL

½ pint mayonnaise
Juice ½ lemon

1 teaspoon Worcestershire
sauce
1 tablespoon tomato ketchup

Place mayonnaise in a mixing bowl and blend in remaining
    ingredients.
Serve with fish.

MOCK HOLLANDAISE SAUCE
Preparation Time: 5 minutes · Cooking Time: NIL

1 egg yolk
2 tablespoons white vinegar

Small can evaporated milk
Salt and pepper

Put ingredients in a basin over a pan of hot water on a gentle
    heat.
Whisk until thick and fluffy.
Serve with asparagus or fish.

QUICK CHOCOLATE TOFFEE SAUCE
Preparation Time: 5 minutes · Cooking Time: NIL

4 tablespoons golden syrup
1½ tablespoons cocoa

1 teaspoon coffee essence

Place all ingredients in a saucepan and heat slowly, stirring
    continuously until simmering.
Pour hot over vanilla ice-cream.

10 minutes

ALMOND CIDER SAUCE

Preparation Time: 10 minutes · Cooking Time: NIL

1 egg	½ oz. ground almonds
2 teaspoons cornflour	1-2 teaspoons sugar
½ pint cider	

Beat together the egg and cornflour.

Heat the cider and pour it onto the egg mixture, stirring all the time. Return to the pan and stir over heat until the sauce boils and thickens. Add the ground almonds and sugar.

Serve hot with Christmas pudding. A little brandy or rum can be added to the sauce, or a few finely chopped glacé cherries.

BROAD BEAN AND HAM SALAD

Preparation Time: 10 minutes · Cooking Time: NIL

10 oz. can broad beans	Salt and pepper
3 tablespoons olive oil	Pinch mustard
1 tablespoon white vinegar	3 oz. shredded ham

Drain the broad beans and rinse well.

Put the oil into a basin and whisk in the vinegar.

Season with salt and pepper and the mustard.

Stir in the beans with the ham.

Can also be served as a first course.

BUTTERSCOTCH SAUCE

Preparation Time: 10 minutes · Cooking Time: NIL

3 oz. butter	Small can evaporated milk
5 oz. light-brown sugar	½ teaspoon vanilla

Melt the butter in a small saucepan.

Add the sugar and stir over a gentle heat until the sugar has dissolved. Bring to the boil and simmer for 5 minutes. Remove from heat and stir in milk and vanilla.

If not quite smooth, stir over heat until any pieces of butter-scotch have melted.

Serve, hot or cold, with ice-cream.

This is also good with apple-based sweets—fools, fluffs and pies, for instance.

MIXED BEAN SALAD

Preparation Time: 10 minutes · Cooking Time: NIL

1 small onion
1½ tablespoons wine vinegar
3 tablespoons olive oil
Salt and pepper

15½ oz. can butter beans
15 oz. can flageolet beans
Chopped parsley

Peel the onion and chop very finely.

Combine the vinegar and olive oil in a bowl and whisk with a fork.

Add salt and pepper and the chopped onion.

Drain the beans from their liquids, rinse and drain again.

Add beans to the prepared dressing and chop gently.

Serve sprinkled with finely chopped parsley.

Most beans can be used in this salad—fresh, frozen, tinned or dried. Except for tinned beans, they should be cooked in boiling salted water until tender (dried beans having been soaked overnight).

OLIVE PINEAPPLE SLICES

Preparation Time: 10 minutes · Cooking Time: NIL

12 stuffed olives
¼ lb. sultanas
8 oz. cottage cheese

1 tablespoon cream or mayonnaise
6 slices pineapple, fresh or canned

Chop the sultanas and 9 olives, reserving the others for garnishing.

Combine cream cheese, sultanas and olives and moisten with cream or mayonnaise.

Cut the pineapple slices in half horizontally.

Sandwich the split slices with the cheese mixture.

Decorate the centre of each with a halved stuffed olive.
Serve with green salad.

PINEAPPLE AND PEPPER SALAD
Preparation Time: 10 minutes · Cooking Time: NIL

2 green peppers	1-2 tablespoons wine vinegar
16 oz. can pineapple cubes	or lemon juice
French dressing:	2-3 tablespoons olive oil
	Salt and pepper

Halve the peppers and remove pith and seeds. Slice finely.
Drain the pineapple cubes.
Combine the dressing ingredients and whisk with a fork.
Pour over pineapple and peppers in a bowl and toss well.

QUICK BARBECUE SAUCE
Preparation Time: 10 minutes · Cooking Time: NIL

2-3 serving packet tomato soup	2 tablespoons vinegar
¾ pint water	1 teaspoon Worcestershire
2 tablespoons dried onions	sauce

Empty soup into a medium-sized saucepan.
Gradually stir in the water; add remaining ingredients.
Bring to boil. Simmer 5 minutes.
Serve with barbecued meats and grills.

TOSSED APRICOT AND ONION SALAD
Preparation Time: 10 minutes · Cooking Time: NIL

1 onion	2 tablespoons olive oil
1 teaspoon dried mint or 1	15 oz. can apricot halves
tablespoon finely chopped	Black olives
fresh mint	Extra mint
1 tablespoon garlic vinegar	Salt and pepper

Peel the onion and slice very finely, separating the rings.
Combine mint, oil, vinegar, salt and pepper in a jar and shake
well.

Pour this dressing over the onion rings and leave to stand for 5
minutes.
Drain the apricots and cut them into slices.
Combine onion and dressing mixture, apricots and olives in
a salad bowl and toss gently.
Garnish with extra chopped mint.
Serve with cold ham.

15 minutes

AUTUMN SALAD

Preparation Time: 15 minutes · Cooking Time: NIL

16 oz. bag frozen garden peas	Salt, pepper and dry mustard
4 oz. mushrooms	¼ teaspoon caster sugar
2 tablespoons olive oil	1 tablespoon wine vinegar
1 clove garlic	2 sticks celery

Cook the peas in boiling, salted water according to the directions;
drain.
Slice the mushrooms.
Heat the oil in a pan and add the mushrooms. Cook slowly until
soft. Remove from heat and strain, reserving the liquor.
Rub a basin with a cut clove of garlic. If a stronger garlic flavour
is wanted, add a crushed clove.
Add the seasonings, sugar and mushroom liquor and then add
the vinegar slowly.
Wash the celery and slice finely. Mix the celery, mushrooms
and peas with the dressing.
Serve chilled.

BARBECUE SAUCE

Preparation Time: 15 minutes · Cooking Time: NIL

2 oz. butter	2 tablespoons sweet pickle
1 onion, chopped	Pinch dry mustard
2 tablespoons tomato purée	½ pint water
2 tablespoons vinegar	

(This sauce should be made in advance i.e. on the afternoon
  before an evening barbecue.)
Melt butter and fry onion until tender.
Stir in tomato purée, vinegar, pickle and mustard. Gradually
  add water and bring to the boil.
Cook for 5 minutes.
Serve hot or cold with barbecued steaks.

CARROT AND RAISIN SALAD

Preparation Time: 15 minutes · Cooking Time: NIL

½ lb. carrots	1 dessertspoon lemon juice
2 oz. raisins	¼ teaspoon salt
8 oz. can pineapple tidbits	Salad greens
5-6 tablespoons mayonnaise	

Peel and grate the carrots.
Combine with the raisins and drained pineapple.
Blend in mayonnaise, lemon juice and salt.
Serve on crisp salad greens.

CELERY AND APPLE SALAD

Preparation Time: 15 minutes · Cooking Time: NIL

11 oz. can mandarin oranges	1 teaspoon sugar
2 tablespoons olive oil	Small head celery
Salt	2 eating apples
½ teaspoon French mustard	1 chicory (optional)
1 tablespoon mayonnaise	¼ lb. black grapes
1 dessertspoon wine vinegar	

Drain mandarins, reserving syrup. Combine in a small bowl
  2 tablespoons of the mandarin juice, the olive oil, salt,
  mustard, mayonnaise, wine vinegar and sugar.
Whisk until smooth.
Wash and slice the celery; peel, core and slice the apples. Mix
  with the prepared dressing.
Slice the chicory and add to salad with the mandarin segments.
Transfer to a salad bowl and serve garnished with halved,
  pipped black grapes.

COLCANNON

Preparation Time: 15 minutes · Cooking Time: 20 minutes

Cup finely chopped cooked
  cabbage
Cup cold mashed potatoes

Salt and pepper
1 egg, beaten
Browned breadcrumbs

Mix together the cabbage, potatoes, salt and pepper.
In a saucepan, melt a little butter or dripping. Put in the
  cabbage and potato, mixing well.
Stir in the beaten egg.
Grease an ovenproof dish and coat the inside with browned
  breadcrumbs.
Put in it the cabbage mixture and bake at gas mark 5, 375° F.,
  until firm.
Turn out and serve to accompany meat.

ORANGE CHICKEN SALAD

Preparation Time: 15 minutes · Cooking Time: NIL

3 sticks celery
1 lb. cooked, diced chicken
1 teaspoon grated onion
1 teaspoon chopped parsley
1 teaspoon curry powder

¼ pint mayonnaise
10 oz. can mandarin oranges
1 oz. chopped walnuts
Lettuce

Chop the celery, and mix with the chicken, curry powder,
  grated onion, chopped parsley and mayonnaise.
Drain oranges. Mix in carefully.
Serve on a bed of lettuce, sprinkling the chopped walnuts over
  the chicken mixture.

OVEN-BAKED MUSHROOM RICE

Preparation Time: 15 minutes · Cooking Time: 30-40 minutes

1½ oz. butter
8 oz. long grain rice
1 onion
7½ oz. can button mushrooms
2 oz. canned pimentos

1 tablespoon chopped chives or
  1 teaspoon dried chives
¾ pint chicken stock
¼ pint dry sherry
1 teaspoon salt
½ teaspoon pepper

Grease an ovenproof dish with ½ oz. butter. Sprinkle in the rice.

Peel and chop the onion. Melt the remaining butter in a sauté pan and fry the onion gently until soft.

Add the drained mushrooms, 2 fl. oz. of mushroom liquor from the can, the sliced pimentos, chives, chicken, stock, sherry and seasonings. Bring to the boil.

Pour this mixture over the rice and stir. Cover with a tight-fitting lid or foil.

Bake in a moderate oven, gas mark 5, 375° F., for 30-40 minutes or until rice is tender and liquid absorbed.

Serve as a vegetable with poultry.

POTATO SALAD

Preparation Time: 15 minutes · Cooking Time: NIL

2 tablespoons instant salad onions
17½ oz. can diced potatoes
3 hardboiled eggs

¼ pint mayonnaise
Salt and pepper
Flaked browned almonds

Reconstitute the salad onions according to directions on pack; drain.

Drain the potatoes.

Remove shells from eggs and chop roughly, add to the potatoes with the onions, mayonnaise and seasoning to taste. Toss gently but thoroughly.

Transfer to a serving dish and sprinkle with the almonds.

QUICK CHESTNUT AND SAUSAGEMEAT STUFFING

Preparation Time: 15 minutes · Cooking Time: NIL

1 onion
1 oz. butter
Turkey liver
½ lb. pork sausagemeat

15½ oz. can unsweetened chestnut purée
2 oz. fresh white breadcrumbs
2 tablespoons chopped parsley
Salt and pepper

Peel and chop the onion finely. Sauté in the butter until transparent.

Chop the turkey liver and add to onion. Toss in the hot fat for a minute or two.

Combine sausagemeat, chestnut purée and the breadcrumbs in a basin. Add the onion and liver mixture, the chopped parsley and a generous amount of seasoning.

Mix all together well and stuff into turkey before roasting.

QUICK CHUTNEY

Preparation Time: 15 minutes · Cooking Time: NIL

3 tablespoons piquant sauce
1 tablespoon tomato purée
7½ oz. can apple sauce
2 eating apples

1 banana
2 oz. raisins
½ oz. chopped walnuts
½ oz. nibbed almonds

Blend together the piquant sauce, tomato purée and apple sauce.

Peel and core the apples, chop roughly.

Peel and chop the banana.

Add fruit and nuts to sauce mixture and mix thoroughly.

Spoon into screw-top jars and store in the refrigerator.

This sauce will keep for up to 2 weeks.

Serve with cold meats and poultry.

SALADE NIÇOISE

Preparation Time: 15 minutes · Cooking Time: NIL

8 oz. packet frozen French beans
7 oz. can tuna
2 hardboiled eggs
2 tomatoes

Few anchovy fillets
Black olives
1 tablespoon wine vinegar
3 tablespoons olive oil
Salt and pepper

Cook the beans in boiling, salted water. Drain and refresh under cold tap. Leave to cool completely.

Drain and flake the tuna.

Shell the hard-boiled eggs and cut into quarters. Cut the tomatoes into quarters.

Cut the anchovy fillets into thin strips.

Combine the vinegar and olive oil in a small bowl and whisk with a fork. Add salt and pepper to taste.

Place the beans and tuna in a salad bowl. Pour over the oil and vinegar dressing and toss well.

Arrange the quartered eggs and tomatoes on top with the anchovy strips and a few black olives scattered over them.

SWEET CIDER JELLY

Preparation Time: 15 minutes · Cooking Time: NIL

2 pints sweet cider	8 fl. oz. bottle liquid fruit
3¼ lb. sugar (preferably pre-	pectin
serving sugar)	

Put the cider and sugar into a large saucepan and mix well. Stir over a gentle heat until the sugar has dissolved.

Add the liquid fruit pectin and bring mixture to a full rolling boil. Boil hard for 1 minute.

Remove pan from heat and take off any scum that has formed on the surface, using a teaspoon. This is important in order to keep the jelly clear.

Pour into hot, clean jam jars and fill to within ¼ inch of the top.

Place a round of waxed paper on surface of jelly. Moisten one side of the cellophane jam pot covers and place, damp side up, on top of pots, securing with an elastic band round the neck.

The cover, in drying, will contract to give a tight seal.

Attach a label to the side of the jar with the name of the jelly and the month in which it was made.

This jelly is delicious on buttered toast, or with ham.

Makes about 5½ lb. jelly.

WINTER SALAD

Preparation Time: 15 minutes · Cooking Time: NIL

6 oz. quick-cooking macaroni	1 small white cabbage or ½
1 eating apple	large white cabbage
2 sticks celery	2 oz. chopped walnuts
2 oz. carrots	2 oz. raisins
	About ¼ pint mayonnaise

Cook the macaroni in boiling, salted water as directed. Drain and rinse thoroughly.
While the macaroni is cooking, peel, core and chop the apple. Wash and chop the celery. Peel and chop the carrots. Wash and shred the cabbage.
Combine all the ingredients in a large bowl and mix thoroughly.
Serves 6.

20 minutes

CRISPY VEGETABLES

Preparation Time: 20 minutes · Cooking Time: NIL

1 small cauliflower
2 sticks celery
1 onion
2 oz. butter

½ teaspoon chicken stock powder
¼ pint dry white wine
Salt and pepper

Break the cauliflower into flowerets.
Slice the celery and peel and slice the onion.
Melt the butter in a saucepan. Add the vegetables, wine, stock and seasoning.
Cook quickly, stirring frequently, for 10 minutes or until vegetables are tender but still crisp, being careful not to overcook them.
Adjust seasoning and serve hot.

FRENCH BEANS WITH TOMATO SAUCE

Preparation Time: 20 minutes · Cooking Time: NIL

1 onion
1 oz. butter
2 rashers streaky bacon
8 oz. can tomatoes
⅛ teaspoon instant garlic powder
1 bayleaf

Sprig of parsley or ½ teaspoon dried parsley
Salt and pepper
8 oz. packet frozen French beans
2 tablespoons grated cheese

Peel and slice the onion, sauté in the butter for a few minutes, then add the de-rinded bacon, cut into strips.

When onion is soft, add the tomatoes, garlic, bayleaf, parsley and seasoning.

Bring to the boil, cover and simmer for 10 minutes.

Meanwhile, cook the French beans in boiling, salted water according to directions on pack. Drain and arrange in a heat-proof dish.

Remove bayleaf and parsley sprig (unless dried parsley is used) from the sauce, adjust seasoning and spoon sauce over the beans.

Sprinkle the grated cheese over the sauce and brown under a hot grill.

KASHMIRI RICE

Preparation Time: 20 minutes · Cooking Time: NIL

6 oz. long-grain rice	1 teaspoon powdered ginger
2 onions	Chili powder to taste
2 oz. butter	3 oz. desiccated coconut
1 clove garlic	3 oz. cashew nuts
7½ oz. can tomatoes	Two 5 fl. oz. cartons natural
1½ teaspoons salt	unsweetened yoghurt
¼ teaspoon pepper	

Cook the rice according to directions on the packet.

Peel and chop the onions. Melt the butter in a sauté pan, add the onion and cook until tender without allowing it to colour.

Add the crushed garlic, drained and chopped tomatoes, seasoning, spices and rice; then the coconut and half the cashews. Mix gently but thoroughly over a gentle heat.

Fold in yoghurt.

Heat through but do not allow yoghurt to become too hot or it will curdle.

Top with remaining nuts.

Serve with roast chicken.

VEGETABLE HOT POT

Preparation Time: 20 minutes · Cooking Time: 30 minutes

1 medium-sized cabbage (about 1 lb.)	2 large onions (sliced)
½ lb. carrots, peeled	4 oz. butter
1 lb. potatoes (peeled)	Salt and pepper
	½ level tablespoon mixed herbs

Slice cabbage thinly and cook in boiling, salted water for 5 minutes. Drain.

Cut potatoes and carrots into ¼-inch slices and cook in boiling salted water for 5-7 minutes. Drain.

Fry onions in 2 oz. butter until tender but not browned.

Use 1 oz. of remaining butter to grease an ovenproof casserole.

Arrange cabbage, carrots, onion and potatoes in layers with seasonings and herbs in casserole dish.

Finish with potato, dot remaining 1 oz. butter over potato and bake in a hot oven, gas mark 7, 425° F., for 30 minutes until browned.

Puddings/Sweets

Puddings/Sweets - 5 minutes

APRICOT AND WALNUT WHIP
Preparation Time: 5 minutes · Cooking Time: NIL

7¾ oz. can apricot halves
¼ pint double cream
2 oz. chopped walnuts

1 oz. icing sugar
A little vanilla

Drain the apricots and slice or chop them.
Whip the cream lightly, fold in icing sugar and vanilla, then
    stir in apricots and walnuts.
Spoon into 4 small glasses.

APRICOT FLARED
Preparation Time: 5 minutes · Cooking Time: NIL

1 lb. 13 oz. can apricot halves
Finely grated peel of 1 medium
    orange

6 tablespoons rum
¼ pint double cream, lightly
    whipped

Put apricots, syrup from can and orange peel into a saucepan.
Bring just up to boil.
Meanwhile, warm rum in a small pan. Set light to it and pour
    immediately over the apricots.
Serve at once with whipped cream.

ICE-CREAM AND CURAÇOA
Preparation Time: 5 minutes · Cooking Time: NIL

¼ pint double cream
1 tablespoon Curaçoa
1 family block vanilla ice-cream

1 teaspoon cinnamon
Sponge fingers

Whip the cream until thick. Fold in the Curaçoa.
Scoop the ice-cream into 6 glass dishes. Sprinkle it with cin-
    namon.
Top with a whirl of the flavoured cream.
Serve with sponge fingers.

PEARS IN BRANDY

Preparation Time: 5 minutes · Cooking Time: NIL

8 canned pear halves, drained   ¼ pint brandy
2 tablespoons icing sugar

Arrange pears on a warm dish. Sprinkle with icing sugar.
Warm the brandy very carefully. It must not be hot, just warm.
Ignite, pour over pears, and serve.

10 minutes

APPLE AND MARSHMALLOW SWEET

Preparation Time: 10 minutes · Cooking Time: NIL

5½ oz. packet marshmallows   ¼ teaspoon cinnamon
10½ oz. jar apple sauce   1 teaspoon lemon juice

Cut the marshmallows into small pieces and place all but about
   ½ oz. in a saucepan with the apple sauce and cinnamon.
Heat gently, stirring, until the marshmallows have dissolved.
Remove from heat and stir in lemon juice.
Spoon into a serving dish and scatter reserved chopped marsh-
   mallows over top.
Other kinds of fruit, puréed, can be used.

APPLEBERRY

Preparation Time: 10 minutes · Cooking Time: NIL

Half of one pint packet custard   Few drops vanilla
   powder   Little ground cinnamon
½ pint milk   4 fl. oz. packet cream topping
1-2 tablespoons sugar   Extra 4 fl. oz. milk
14 oz. can apple and blackberry
   pie filling

Make custard following directions on packet using ½ pint milk
   and the sugar.
Combine custard and pie filling.

Add vanilla and cinnamon to taste.

Transfer to a serving dish and smooth the top.

Make up cream topping using the extra milk, following directions on packet.

Spread over the blackberry mixture.

If desired, sprinkle with a little extra cinnamon.

Vary this recipe using different pie fillings and suitable spices.

APPLE CREAM

Preparation Time: 10 minutes · Cooking Time: 20 minutes

1 red apple	2 oz. caster sugar
4 fl. oz. double cream	Juice of ½ a lemon

Wash apple and grate coarsely (do not peel).

Whip cream lightly.

Fold in grated apple, sugar and lemon juice.

Put in freezing compartment of refrigerator for 20 minutes before serving.

AVOCADO WITH STRAWBERRIES

Preparation Time: 10 minutes · Cooking Time: NIL

1 avocado	½ lb. fresh or frozen (but
1 tablespoon Cointreau	thawed) strawberries
5 fl. oz. carton hazelnut yoghurt	Grated chocolate

Halve the avocado and remove the stones. Scoop out most of the flesh from both halves and put in a bowl.

Sprinkle the Cointreau over the avocado halves.

Mix the yoghurt with the avocado flesh and add the strawberries, halved. (Retain a few for decoration.)

Mix gently, taking care not to break the strawberries.

Pile into avocado halves and garnish with halved strawberries and grated chocolate.

BAKED BLACKCURRANT PUDDING

Preparation Time: 10 minutes · Cooking Time: 15-20 minutes

14¼ oz. can blackcurrant pie
  filling
3-4 slices white bread

Butter
Caster sugar

Spread the pie filling across the base of a fairly shallow oven-proof dish.

Spread the bread slices with plenty of butter, remove crusts and cut each slice into 4 triangles.

Arrange the bread, butter side up, over the pie filling and bake in a hot oven, gas mark 7, 425° F., for 15-20 minutes, or until bread is crisp and golden brown and filling is bubbling.

Remove from oven, sprinkle lightly with caster sugar and serve hot with cream or custard.

Try making this also with apricot or gooseberry pie fillings.

BAKED PEACHES WITH ALMONDS

Preparation Time: 10 minutes · Cooking Time: 20 minutes

15½ oz. can peach halves
4 macaroons
Grated rind ½ orange
1-2 tablespoons caster sugar

1-2 tablespoons white wine
1 oz. flaked almonds
5 fl. oz. carton natural yoghurt
  or soured cream

Drain peaches, reserving the syrup.

Crush macaroons and mix with grated orange peel, caster sugar and white wine. Using a wooden spoon, press mixture to form a paste. Spoon this filling into the hollows of the peach halves. Sprinkle with flaked almonds.

Arrange the peaches in a buttered ovenproof dish. Bake in a moderate oven, gas mark 4, 350° F., for 20 minutes.

Mix a little of the peach juice with the yoghurt or soured cream and serve as a sauce with the hot peaches.

BANANA AND CHOCOLATE PUDDING

Preparation Time: 10 minutes · Cooking Time: 25-30 minutes

1 heaped teaspoon apricot jam
3 bananas
3 oz. self-raising flour
2 oz. shredded suet

1 oz. chocolate powder or cocoa
2 oz. caster sugar
Milk to mix

Grease an ovenproof dish. Spread the apricot jam in the base.
Peel and slice two of the bananas and arrange on the jam.
Mix together the sifted flour, suet, chocolate or cocoa, and the
  sugar.
Peel the remaining banana and cut into slices. Mash into the
  dry ingredients. Then add enough milk (about 3-4 fl. oz.) to
  make a sticky mixture.
Spoon over bananas and jam in dish.
Bake in a moderate oven, gas mark 5, 375° F., for 25-30 minutes,
  or until pudding is cooked through.
Serve hot.

BLACKCURRANT AND APPLE
SHORTBREAD

Preparation Time: 10 minutes · Cooking Time: 40 minutes

6 oz. packet shortbread mix
3 oz. butter or margarine
½ teaspoon ground ginger

13¾ oz. can apple and blackcurrant pie filling

Make up shortbread mix according to directions on packet,
  using the butter or margarine; stir in ground ginger.
Empty pie filling into an ovenproof dish.
Sprinkle over shortbread mixture and smooth the surface.
Bake in a cool oven, gas mark 2, 300° F., for 40 minutes.
Serve hot.

BLACKBERRY AND MACAROON SUNDAES

Preparation Time: 10 minutes · Cooking Time: NIL

4 macaroons
13½ oz. can blackberries

4 fl. oz. milk
4 fl. oz. packet topping mix

Drain the blackberries and divide evenly between 4 glasses.
Spoon over a little of the syrup.
Crumble a macaroon into each glass to cover blackberries.
Whip the topping mix with the milk and pipe a swirl over each
 sundae.
Serve chilled.

CHOCOLATE APRICOT TRIFLE

Preparation Time: 10 minutes · Cooking Time: NIL

Chocolate Swiss roll
2 tablespoons brandy or rum
14¼ oz. can apricot pie filling

¼ pint double cream
7¾ oz. can apricot halves or a
 milk chocolate flake

Cut the Swiss roll into slices and arrange in base of a serving
 dish.
Sprinkle with brandy or rum.
Spread with apricot pie filling.
Whip the cream lightly and spread across pie filling.
Decorate with drained apricot halves or crumbled milk choco-
 late flake.
For children, replace the brandy or rum with fruit juice.

CHOCOLATE CHIP ICE-CREAM

Preparation Time: 10 minutes · Cooking Time: NIL

1 teaspoon gelatine
Small can evaporated milk
1 teaspoon vanilla essence

3 oz. caster sugar
2 oz. chocolate dots

Soften the gelatine in a little cold water, then dissolve by
 adding 2 tablespoons boiling water.
Whisk the chilled evaporated milk until thick enough to hold
 a trail left by the whisk.
Whisk in vanilla essence, caster sugar, gelatine and chocolate
 dots.
Pour into ice trays and place in the ice-making compartment
 of refrigerator, set at its coldest, until frozen (about 1½-2
 hours).
This ice-cream needs no beating or stirring during freezing.

Ginger Ice-Cream
Make as above, omitting the vanilla essence and chocolate dots, and whisking in 2 tablespoons of chopped stem ginger and a little syrup.

Vanilla Ice-Cream
Make as above, omitting the chocolate dots.

CHOCOLATE MOUSSE

Preparation Time: 10 minutes · Cooking Time: NIL

4 oz. plain chocolate   3 eggs

Break the chocolate into a basin. Stand in a saucepan of hot water until the chocolate has melted.
Do not stir until melted and do not allow the water to become too hot or the chocolate will lose its gloss.
Separate the eggs and stir the melted chocolate into the beaten yolks.
Beat the egg whites stiffly and fold into the chocolate mixture.
Pour into individual dishes and chill until lightly set.
Serve alone or with single cream.

CHOCOLATE RUM PUDDING

Preparation Time: 10 minutes · Cooking Time: 45 minutes

3-4 tablespoons clear honey	2 tablespoons caster sugar
1 oz. flaked almonds	4 tablespoons milk
5 oz. sachet chocolate sponge mix	1 egg
	4 tablespoons rum

Grease a 7-inch cake tin (fixed base) and insert a piece of greased greaseproof paper in the bottom. Spoon in the honey and sprinkle with flaked almonds.
Empty the sponge mix into a mixing bowl and make up, following directions on packet, using the sugar, egg and milk.
Carefully spoon the sponge over the almonds.
Bake in the centre of a moderate oven, gas mark 4, 350° F., for 45 minutes or until cake is done when tested with a skewer.
Turn onto a warm plate and pour the rum over the top.
Serve hot with cream, cream topping or custard.

COFFEE MERINGUE

Preparation Time: 10 minutes · Cooking Time: 2 hours

3 egg whites	½ pint double cream
6 oz. caster sugar	3 tablespoons coffee liqueur

Draw two circles, 8 inches in diameter, on a piece of non-stick baking paper. Place it on a baking sheet.

Whisk the egg whites until very stiff, add 1 teaspoon sugar and whisk again. Fold in remaining sugar.

Spread the meringue mixture lightly and evenly within the two circles. Bake in a slow oven, gas mark ½, 250° F., for about 2 hours. Remove from paper and cool on cooling racks.

Before serving, whip the cream until stiff and fold in the coffee liqueur.

Spread half the cream mixture on one meringue circle, place the other meringue on top. Spread with remaining cream.

Serve cut into slices. Slicing is much simpler if the knife is dipped into hot water between each cut.

COFFEE WHISK

Preparation Time: 10 minutes · Cooking Time: NIL

1 tablespoon gelatine	Large can evaporated milk
1 tablespoon instant coffee	Whipped cream
3-4 oz. caster sugar	Chocolate buttons

Soften the gelatine in 2 tablespoons cold water; then dissolve in 2 tablespoons hot water.

Add the coffee and sugar to taste.

Whisk the chilled evaporated milk until thick, then whisk in the coffee mixture and pour into a dish or small glasses.

Refrigerate until set.

Serve decorated with whipped cream and chocolate buttons.

CRÈME HILDA

Preparation Time: 10 minutes · Cooking Time: 1 hr. 15 min.

16 oz. can stoneless red cherries	3 eggs
Large can evaporated milk	1½ oz. caster sugar

Drain the cherries and arrange them in a greased, round oven-proof dish approximately 6 inches in diameter.

Bring the evaporated milk up to 1 pint with water, and heat to boiling point, pour onto beaten eggs and sugar, stirring well, then pour over cherries and bake in a moderate oven, gas mark 4, 350° F., for approximately 1¼ hours, until just set.

Turn out and serve hot or cold.

CRUNCHY CARAMEL PUDDING

Preparation Time: 10 minutes · Cooking Time: NIL

1 pint packet caramel top dessert mix	1 pint milk
	2 oz. nut brittle

Follow instructions on packet for caramel topping and the mix, using the milk.

Transfer to a mould.

Place nut brittle in a bowl and crush with end of a rolling-pin into smaller pieces; alternatively, use a pestle and mortar.

Sprinkle crushed nut brittle over the pudding. It will sink to the bottom.

Put mould in a cool place and unmould when set.

GOOSEBERRY CRISP

Preparation Time: 10 minutes · Cooking Time: NIL

13¾ oz. can gooseberry pie filling	2 oz. Demerara sugar
2 oz. butter	2 oz. cornflakes

Spread the pie filling across the base of a fairly flat, heat-proof dish.

Cream the butter and sugar and mix in the cornflakes.

Sprinkle over the filling and grill for 2-3 minutes.

Serve with cream or custard.

GOOSEBERRY CRUMBLE CREAM

Preparation Time: 10 minutes · Cooking Time: 40 minutes

13¾ oz. can gooseberry pie
   filling
Small can sweetened condensed
   milk

Juice 1 lemon
8 oz. packet crumble mix

Empty the pie filling into a basin. Stir in the lemon juice, then
  add the condensed milk. Mix gently but thoroughly. Transfer
  to a 1½ pint pie dish.
Sprinkle the crumble mix over the top of the fruit, rubbing out
  any lumps with your fingertips. Press down gently.
Bake in a moderately hot oven, gas mark 6, 400° F., for 40
  minutes, or until crumble is golden.
Serve warm or hot.

GRADDTARTA

Preparation Time: 10 minutes · Cooking Time: NIL

½ pint double cream
½ lb. broken biscuits

4 oz. jam

Whip the cream until thick.
Spread broken biscuits with the jam, and layer the biscuits and
  the cream in a serving bowl.
Chill and serve topped with piped jam.

GRAPE BRÛLÉE

Preparation Time: 10 minutes · Cooking Time: NIL

14 oz. can peeled Muscat grapes
¼ pint double cream

1½ oz. Demerara sugar

Preheat grill (hottest setting).
Drain grapes and arrange in the base of a fairly shallow fire-
  proof dish.
Whip the cream lightly and spread over grapes. Dust with
  Demerara sugar.

Place under the hot grill and cook until cream bubbles and sugar
has caramelised.
Serve immediately.
Delicious, too, with strawberries: sprinkle with sugar first, if
wanted.

HONEYED FIGS

Preparation Time: 10 minutes · Cooking Time: NIL

20 oz. can green figs
3 tablespoons honey

¼ pint fresh or canned unsweetened orange juice

Drain the figs.
Combine honey and orange juice in a saucepan. Bring to the
boil and boil fairly rapidly until mixture has reduced and
become syrupy.
Lower heat so syrup simmers. Add the figs and heat through.
Arrange figs in a serving dish and pour over syrup.
Serve hot or cold, with cream.

HONEYED RAISIN PUDDING

Preparation Time: 10 minutes · Cooking Time: 35 minutes

2 tablespoons honey
½ oz. butter
4 fl. oz. milk
1 oz. breadcrumbs

4 oz. seedless raisins
2 oz. chopped mixed nuts
½ teaspoon cinnamon
1 teaspoon baking powder

Heat together honey, milk and butter until honey has dissolved
and butter melted. Do not allow to become too hot.
Place breadcrumbs, raisins and nuts in a greased ovenproof
dish.
Add cinnamon and baking powder to the milk mixture and
stir into dry ingredients.
Bake in a moderate oven, gas mark 4, 350° F., for 35 minutes.
Serve warm or cold with whipped cream or ice-cream.

ICED ORANGE CUPS

Preparation Time: 10 minutes · Cooking Time: NIL

2 large oranges
17 fl. oz. brick orange ripple
  ice-cream

Little whipped cream

Cut the oranges in half and, using a grapefruit knife, remove the flesh and put on one side.

Spoon out any juice and pulp remaining in the shells and place upside down to drain.

Spoon some slightly-softened ice-cream into the orange halves and level off top using the back of a knife.

Cover with a small piece of greaseproof paper and aluminium foil and place in freezing compartment of refrigerator or deep freeze until needed.

If the cups are not quite level, cut a small piece of peel off the base.

Using a sharp knife, cut the flesh from the reserved orange segments, trying to keep them as complete as possible as they are used later for decoration.

Before serving the orange cups, quickly pipe a swirl of whipped cream in the centre of each one and arrange some orange segments round the edge.

LEMON CRUNCH CREAMS

Preparation Time: 10 minutes · Cooking Time: NIL

¼ pint double cream
Small can sweetened condensed
  milk

Juice and grated rind of 1
  lemon
Packet brandy snaps

Stir the lemon rind and juice into the condensed milk.
Fold in the lightly whipped cream.
Half-fill four small, stemmed glasses with the lemon mixture, arranging a layer of crumbled brandy snaps on top.
Cover with remaining lemon cream.
Chill.
Before serving, crumble a brandy snap over each lemon cream.

MACARONI MILK PUDDING
Preparation Time: 10 minutes · Cooking Time: NIL

1 heaped dessertspoon corn-flour	3 oz. quick-cooking macaroni
1 pint milk	1 oz. granulated sugar
1½ oz. butter	1 oz. Demerara sugar
	Little grated nutmeg

Blend cornflour with a little milk. Put remaining milk and 1 oz. butter on to boil.

Add macaroni and simmer for 7 minutes. Stir in blended corn-flour, add the granulated sugar and simmer for 2-3 minutes, stirring all the time.

Pour into ovenproof dish, sprinkle with Demerara sugar and nutmeg, and dot with remaining butter.

Brown under a hot grill.

MARSHMALLOW ICE-CREAM
Preparation Time: 10 minutes · Cooking Time: NIL

½ lb. marshmallows	2 heaped teaspoons malted milk granules
¼ pint milk	
¼ pint double cream	1 oz. chopped nuts

Set refrigerator at its coldest.

Melt the marshmallows in the hot milk; cool.

Whip cream lightly.

Combine all ingredients. Pour mixture into freezing trays and freeze until firm.

MERINGUED FRUIT SPONGE
Preparation Time: 10 minutes · Cooking Time: 20 minutes

1 jam Swiss roll	15 oz. can plums, greengages or other fruit
2 egg whites	
4 oz. caster sugar	

Cut Swiss roll into slices and line the bottom and sides of an ovenproof dish.

Heat fruit in pan, then drain and place over Swiss roll.

Whisk egg whites till stiff, then whisk in half the sugar.

Fold in most of the remaining sugar.

Pile meringue over the fruit and sprinkle the remaining sugar on top.

Bake in a moderate oven, gas mark 4 or 350° F., until crisp and lightly coloured.

Serve hot.

ORCHARD RICE

Preparation Time: 10 minutes · Cooking Time: NIL

2½ oz. packet lemon-flavoured dried apple dessert mix

15½ oz. can creamed rice milk pudding

2 tablespoons apricot jam

Chopped walnuts

Make up the apple dessert following directions on the packet.

Mix with creamed rice and apricot jam (if the jam is thick it may be necessary to melt it slightly before adding to rice mixture).

Serve sprinkled with chopped nuts.

PEACH AND MINCEMEAT PIE

Preparation Time: 10 minutes · Cooking Time: 30 minutes

13 oz. packet frozen but thawed shortcrust pastry

8½ oz. can sliced peaches

Half 14½ oz. jar mincemeat

Beaten egg

Roll out the thawed pastry on a lightly-floured board to a rectangle approximately 10 inches by 18 inches.

Cut off enough to line into a 7-inch flan ring, leaving the remainder for the pie top.

Drain the peaches from their syrup and arrange in the base of the flan. Spread the mincemeat over the top.

Cover with the pastry lid, trimming the edges and sealing firmly.

Brush with beaten egg and make a hole in the centre to allow the steam to escape.

If liked, use pastry trimmings, cut into leaf shapes, to decorate

the pie. Brush them with beaten egg, and arrange in place.
Bake in a moderately hot oven, gas mark 6, 400° F., for 30
minutes or until pastry is golden.
Serve hot or cold.

PINEAPPLE GINGER COUPE

Preparation Time: 10 minutes · Cooking Time: NIL

16 oz. can pineapple cubes	2 pieces stem ginger
15½ oz. can melon cubes	2 tablespoons ginger syrup
2 bananas	2 tablespoons lemon juice

Strain pineapple and melon from their syrups. Combine the
syrups and reserve ¼ pint, adding the ginger syrup to the
reserved liquid.
Peel and slice the bananas and turn in the lemon juice.
Combine halved pineapple cubes, melon cubes and sliced
bananas in a bowl. Add chopped ginger.
Pour the reserved syrup over the fruit and chill until flavours
are well-blended.
Spoon into glasses and serve with whipped cream.

PINEAPPLE HONEY CAKE

Preparation Time: 10 minutes · Cooking Time: NIL

Dutch honey cake	1 oz. icing sugar
Three 2oz. portions cream cheese	Maraschino cherries
	Browned flaked almonds
8½ oz. can crushed pineapple	

Slice the honey cake lengthwise into three.
Mix together the cream cheese and sifted icing sugar and beat
well. Add drained pineapple.
Spread two slices with some of this mixture, leaving about a
third for the top.
Reassemble cake and spread remaining cheese and pineapple
mixture over the top.
Decorate with drained, halved maraschino cherries and browned
flaked almonds.

PINEAPPLE SOUR CREAM CAKE
Preparation Time: 10 minutes · Cooking Time: 40 minutes

10 digestive biscuits
Four 5 fl. oz. cartons soured
cream

13¼ oz. can crushed pineapple
4 oz. caster sugar

Using an electric blender, turn the digestive biscuits to crumbs. Alternatively, place biscuits in a plastic bag, and, holding the opening in one hand, crush the biscuits with the end of a rolling pin.

Place biscuit crumbs in the base of a 7½-inch cake tin with a removable base.

Drain the pineapple and mix fruit with the soured cream and caster sugar. Spoon carefully over biscuit crumbs.

Bake in a moderate oven, gas mark 4, 350° F., for 40 minutes.

Remove from oven. When completely cold, refrigerate, preferably overnight.

Decorate with halved pineapple rings. Serve cut into wedges.

RASPBERRY CREAM
Preparation Time: 10 minutes · Cooking Time: NIL

15 oz. can raspberries
6 oz. carton raspberry yoghurt

4 oz. carton double cream
1 egg white

Drain raspberries from their juice and mix the fruit gently with the yoghurt, keeping a few whole raspberries for decoration.

Whip the cream until fairly stiff, whisk the egg white stiffly.

Fold cream and egg white into raspberry mixture, reserving a little cream for decoration.

Transfer to a serving dish, or individual dishes, and decorate with piped cream and reserved raspberries.

RASPBERRY DUMPLINGS

Preparation Time: 10 minutes · Cooking Time: 30 minutes

13½ oz. can raspberries
6 oz. self-raising flour
1 teaspoon baking powder

3 oz. margarine
4½ tablespoons milk
6 oz. golden syrup

Drain the raspberries, reserving the syrup.
Place fruit in the base of a deep ovenproof dish.
Measure the raspberry juice and make up to ½ pint with water.
Sift the flour and baking powder into a basin. Rub in the margarine until the mixture resembles fine breadcrumbs. Mix to a soft dough with the milk.
Divide dough into 8 pieces, lightly form into balls and arrange on raspberries.
Combine golden syrup and raspberry juice in a saucepan and bring to the boil. Pour over the dumplings, cover and bake in a hot oven, gas mark 8, 450° F., for 30 minutes.
Serve hot with cream or custard.

SHERRY WHISK

Preparation Time: 10 minutes · Cooking Time: NIL

8 sponge finger biscuits
2-3 tablespoons sweet sherry
2 egg yolks

1 oz. caster sugar
¼ pint double cream
1 egg white

Crumble four of the biscuits and moisten with a tablespoon of the sherry. Arrange in the bases of 4 small stemmed glasses.
Whisk egg yolks with sugar until pale and fluffy.
Whisk cream and egg white to a soft peak.
Fold remaining sherry and the egg yolk mixture into cream.
Pour over the biscuits in the glasses; chill.
Serve with remaining sponge fingers.

SPICED PEACH SUNDAES

Preparation Time: 10 minutes · Cooking Time: NIL

15½ oz. can sliced peaches
½ oz. butter

½ level teaspoon powdered
cinnamon
1 family brick coffee ice-cream

Strain the fruit, reserving the juice. Melt the butter in a frying-pan until bubbling but not brown.

Add peaches and fry gently, without browning, turning frequently.

Remove from heat, sprinkle cinnamon over them and stir in 5 tablespoons of peach juice.

Reheat gently until juice thickens slightly.

Cut ice-cream into portions and put in individual glasses.

Spoon peaches over ice-cream and serve immediately.

STRAWBERRIES CARDINAL

Preparation Time: 10 minutes · Cooking Time: NIL

Two 8 oz. packets frozen
strawberries
2 tablespoons caster sugar
3 tablespoons raspberry jam

2 tablespoons water
1 teaspoon lemon juice
Browned flaked almonds

Sprinkle strawberries with the sugar and leave to thaw.

Heat the jam with the water in a small saucepan until the jam has melted.

Remove from heat and stir in lemon juice. Cool.

Pile the thawed strawberries into glasses, spoon over the raspberry syrup and serve topped with browned, flaked almonds.

STRAWBERRY YOGHURT MOUSSE

Preparation Time: 10 minutes · Cooking Time: NIL

2 packets red jelly glaze
2 eggs
2 oz. caster sugar

Two 6 oz. cartons strawberry
yoghurt

Make up the jelly glaze as directed on packet, and allow to cool slightly.

Separate eggs and beat the yolks with the sugar.
Stir in yoghurt and jelly glaze.
Whisk egg whites stiffly and fold carefully into yoghurt mixture.
Spoon into individual dishes and chill until set.

STUFFED PEARS

Preparation Time: 10 minutes · Cooking Time: NIL

1 lb. 13 oz. can pear halves	¼ pint double cream
4 oz. raisins	1 oz. glacé cherries, chopped
2 tablespoons rum	1 oz. angelica, chopped

Drain the pears.
Bring the rum with the raisins to the boil in a small saucepan.
   Remove from heat.
Leave until cool.
Whisk cream lightly, stir in the raisins, cherries and angelica.
Pile into pear hollows.
Chill before serving.

SUNNY ORANGE SHERBET

Preparation Time: 10 minutes · Cooking Time: NIL

Small can evaporated milk	6¼ oz. can frozen concentrated
Juice 1 lemon	orange juice
4 oz. caster sugar	11 oz. can mandarin oranges

Set refrigerator at its coldest.
Whip chilled evaporated milk until stiff; add lemon juice while
   still whipping, then the sugar.
Fold in the slightly thawed orange juice.
Pour into ice trays or individual moulds and freeze in the ice-
   making compartment for 2 hours or until solid.
Serve with drained mandarin oranges, or fresh oranges, peeled
   and sliced.

VELVET AMBROSIA

Preparation Time: 10 minutes · Cooking Time: NIL

Small can chilled evaporated milk
1 teaspoon lemon juice

2 tablespoons golden syrup
15½ oz. can fruit cocktail
10 marshmallows

Whip the chilled milk and the lemon juice until stiff.
Gradually beat in the golden syrup.
Drain the fruit cocktail and fold in gently.
Cut the marshmallows into small pieces. Add to mixture.
Serve at once.

15 minutes

APPLE AND CHOCOLATE SWEET

Preparation Time: 15 minutes · Cooking Time: NIL

3-4 servings packet lemon-flavoured apple dessert mix
4 oz. fresh breadcrumbs
2 oz. butter
1 oz. caster sugar

Raspberry jam
¼ pint double cream
1 egg white
Chocolate flakes

Make up the apple dessert with boiling water, following directions on packet. Cool.
Melt the butter in a heavy frying-pan. Add the crumbs and sugar and cook very gently, stirring frequently with a fork, until crisp and pale gold. Cool on absorbent kitchen paper.
Place a spoonful of the buttered crumbs in the base of 4 individual glasses. Top with a little raspberry jam.
Spread apple over. Top with remaining crumbs.
Whisk cream and egg white together till the mixture forms soft peaks. Spread over the crumb layer.
Decorate with small pieces of chocolate flake.
Serve chilled.

APPLE TURNOVERS
Preparation Time: 15 minutes · Cooking Time: 10-15 minutes

½ of 3-4 serving packet orange-flavoured dried apple dessert mix

13 oz. packet puff pastry
Little caster sugar

Make up the apple dessert mix using 6 fl. oz. boiling water, but otherwise following directions on packet.

Roll out the thawed pastry thinly on a lightly-floured board. Cut into 4-inch squares.

Place a heaped teaspoon of the slightly cooled apple on centre of each pastry square, damp edges with water and fold over to form a triangle.

Seal edges firmly. Brush one side of the triangles with water and sprinkle with caster sugar. Place on a baking sheet.

Bake in a hot oven, gas mark 7, 425° F., for 10-15 minutes, or until pastry is golden and cooked through.

Serve warm or cold with cream or apricot sauce.

Makes 6. This recipe can also make one large turnover.

APRICOT FOOL
Preparation Time: 15 minutes · Cooking Time: NIL

Half of 1 pint envelope custard powder
½ pint milk
2-3 tablespoons sugar

14¼ oz. can apricot pie filling
Juice ½ lemon
¼ pint double cream

Make up the custard using the milk and sugar according to directions on pack. This amount of sugar will make a sweet custard.

Sieve or liquidise the pie filling and add lemon juice, stir into custard and allow to cool slightly.

Whip cream lightly, reserving a little for decoration, and fold into apricot and custard mixture.

Transfer to a serving dish, or individual dishes, and chill.

Serve decorated with the reserved whipped cream. If desired, drained canned apricots may be included as decoration.

APRICOT PUFFS
Preparation Time: 15 minutes · Cooking Time: NIL

Beaten egg or milk to glaze
12 uncooked frozen but
   thawed vol-au-vent cases

¾ pint custard made from
   custard powder
2-3 tablespoons apricot jam
½ teaspoon vanilla

Glaze and cook the thawed vol-au-vent cases according to directions on pack.

Cool, and remove any uncooked pastry from the centres, using a teaspoon.

Stir the jam into the hot custard and flavour with vanilla.

When cool, spoon into the pastry cases and top with a drained apricot half, or with the pastry lid.

BANANA WALNUT CAKE
Preparation Time: 15 minutes · Cooking Time: NIL

1 frozen dairy cream sponge
2 bananas
Juice ½ lemon

1 dessertspoon caster sugar
1 oz. chopped walnuts

Cut top layer of sponge from thawed cake (dividing cream equally between both sections) and place on a plate, cut surface up.

Peel bananas. Slice ¾ of one into rings and toss in a little lemon juice. Mash remainder with 1 tablespoon of lemon juice and the sugar. Stir in half the walnuts.

Spread over lower portion of sponge and cover with other half, cream side up: smooth cream.

Arrange banana rings round edge of cake and then sprinkle on the nuts.

BANANAS IN PASTRY
Preparation Time: 15 minutes · Cooking Time: 20-30 minutes

13 oz. packet frozen but
   thawed puff pastry
6 small bananas

Juice of ½ lemon
3 oz. caster sugar

Roll out the thawed pastry to a strip 24 inches long.

Cut into 6 long strips.

Peel the bananas and brush with lemon juice.

Brush the pastry strips with water and sprinkle on two-thirds of the sugar. Wrap pastry around bananas, having sugar side next to fruit. Glaze tops with a little water and the remaining sugar.

Place on a baking sheet and bake at gas mark 6, 400° F., for 20-30 minutes, or until pastry is golden and cooked.

Serve with cream or melted apricot jam.

BILBERRY MALLOW FLAN

Preparation Time: 15 minutes · Cooking Time: NIL

3-4 serving packet bilberry-flavoured dried apple dessert	7-8 inch sponge flan case
	2-3 oz. marshmallows

Make up the apple dessert using water as directed on the packet. Allow to cool.

Place flan case on grill rack and fill with apple.

Arrange marshmallows round edge of filling to form a circle, alternating the pink and white colours.

Place under a hot grill until marshmallows turn pale gold.

BREAD AND BUTTER PUDDING

Preparation Time: 15 minutes · Cooking Time: 45 minutes

4 large slices buttered bread or 6 smaller slices	2 eggs
1 oz. glacé cherries	3 tablespoons caster sugar
½ oz. sultanas	½ teaspoon vanilla
½ oz. currants	Small can evaporated milk
	Grated nutmeg

Remove crusts from buttered bread and cut into triangles.

Cut the glacé cherries into quarters.

Arrange bread and butter, cherries, sultanas and currants in layers in a greased 1½ pint ovenproof dish.

Lightly beat eggs, sugar and vanilla.

Make the evaporated milk up to ¾ pint with hot water and pour onto egg mixture, stirring well. Pour over the bread mixture and leave to stand for 10 minutes.

Sprinkle with grated nutmeg, and stand dish in a baking tin containing warm water.

Bake in a moderately slow oven, gas mark 3, 325° F., for about 45 minutes or until mixture is lightly set.

BUTTERSCOTCH AND COFFEE FLAN

Preparation Time: 15 minutes · Cooking Time: NIL

Sponge flan case
¼ pint double cream
1 teaspoon caster sugar
2 teaspoons instant coffee granules
1 teaspoon hot water
Packet butterscotch-flavoured instant dessert mix
½ pint cold milk

Place flan case on a serving dish. Whisk the cream and sugar until it will hold a peak.

Dissolve the coffee in the hot water and fold into whipped cream.

Make up the butterscotch dessert, using the milk as directed on the packet. Fold half the coffee-flavoured cream into the dessert and spoon into flan case.

Fill remaining coffee cream into a piping bag with a rosette nozzle and use to decorate the flan.

BUTTERSCOTCH PECAN ICE-CREAM

Preparation Time: 15 minutes · Cooking Time: NIL

1 oz. butter
2 oz. light-brown sugar
2 oz. pecan pieces
4 fl. oz. packet cream topping
4 fl. oz. milk
1 egg white

Melt the butter in a saucepan, add the sugar and stir over a gentle heat until the sugar has dissolved. Bring to the boil and boil for 1 minute.

Remove from heat and stir in pecan pieces. The mixture should be of a fudge-like consistency.

Leave to cool while making up topping, following directions on packet and using the 4 oz. of milk.

Whisk the egg white stiffly. Fold into the topping with the butterscotch and nut mixture.

Spoon into freezing trays and freeze until firm.

CARAMEL FRUIT RING
Preparation Time: 15 minutes · Cooking Time: NIL

3 oz. crisp cornflakes
4 oz. soft brown sugar
½ oz. butter
2 oz. golden syrup

2 tablespoons water
Fresh or canned fruit or ice-cream

Brush a 7½-inch ring mould with a little salad oil, or use a 7-inch cake tin with an oiled tumbler in the centre. An 8-inch flan can also be used.

Put the cereal into a large mixing bowl and the remaining ingredients into a thick saucepan.

Heat ingredients gently until the sugar has dissolved, then boil until a little of the mixture forms a soft ball when tested in cold water.

Pour mixture over the cereal, mixing quickly with a fork until the flakes are evenly coated. Press lightly into the prepared mould and leave to set.

To serve: turn out and fill centre with fresh or tinned fruit or with ice-cream.

CARAMEL RICE PUDDING
Preparation Time: 15 minutes · Cooking Time: 1 hour

15½ oz. can rice milk pudding
2 egg yolks
½ teaspoon vanilla

3 oz. sugar
3 tablespoons water

Mix together the rice pudding, beaten egg yolks and vanilla. Place the sugar and water in a thick saucepan. Stir over a gentle heat until the sugar has dissolved.

Raise heat and boil quickly until sugar caramelises and becomes a golden brown. Watch the pan carefully as, once it begins to change colour, the caramel browns very quickly and can burn.

Wrap a tea towel round a loaf tin measuring 7¾ inches by 4 inches. Pour in the caramel. Quickly tilt the tin so sides and base are well-coated.

Spoon rice mixture into caramel-coated tin. Stand in a baking
dish containing hot water.

Cover with aluminium foil and bake in a moderate oven, gas
mark 4, 350° F., until set—about 1 hour.

Allow to cool completely then refrigerate overnight.

Unmould onto a serving dish.

CHESTNUT AND CHOCOLATE CREAMS

Preparation Time: 15 minutes · Cooking Time: NIL

2 eggs
4 oz. sugar
2 oz. chocolate dots
15 oz. can unsweetened chestnut purée

½ teaspoon vanilla
1 dessertspoon rum
¼ pint double cream

Separate eggs. Place yolks in a bowl with the sugar and beat
until light and fluffy.

Place chocolate dots in a basin over a saucepan of hot water and
heat gently until melted.

Sieve chestnut purée. Beat into egg mixture with the vanilla.

Stir in the melted chocolate and the rum.

Whip the cream lightly and the egg whites stiffly.

Fold cream and egg whites alternately into the chestnut mixture.

Transfer to a serving-dish or 4 individual dishes.

Decorate with whirls of whipped cream and *marrons glacés*,
or with chocolate sauce squeezed in a swirling design from
a tube.

CHESTNUT CREAM

Preparation Time: 15 minutes · Cooking Time: NIL

4 tablespoons sweetened chestnut purée
1 tablespoon coffee liqueur
(optional)

½ pint double cream
2 egg whites

Combine purée and liqueur (if used).

Fold in lightly whipped cream, reserving 2 tablespoons cream
for decoration.

Whisk egg whites stiffly and fold into chestnut mixture.
Pour into glasses. Decorate with reserved cream.
Serve with ratafia biscuits or wafers.

CHESTNUT REFRIGERATOR CAKE

Preparation Time: 15 minutes · Cooking Time: NIL

4 oz. unsalted butter
2 oz. caster sugar
1 egg yolk
15½ oz. can unsweetened chestnut purée
2 tablespoons cocoa

2 teaspoons instant coffee
  powder
Brandy or rum to taste
About 15 plain chocolate-
  coated biscuits
Whipped cream

Cream the butter and sugar until light and fluffy. Add the egg
  yolk, beating well, then the chestnut purée.
Add the sifted cocoa and the coffee powder, then the brandy or
  rum. Beat well.
Line the base of a 6½-inch cake tin with greaseproof paper, and
  oil the sides of the tin.
Spoon in the chestnut mixture. Cover tin with aluminium foil
  and refrigerate for 24 hours before unmoulding onto a plate.
Trim the chocolate biscuits to the height of the cake and press
  them round the sides. Decorate top and round the base with
  piped whipped cream.

CHOCOLATE AND PEAR PIE

Preparation Time: 15 minutes · Cooking Time: NIL

½ lb. plain chocolate digestive
  biscuits
3 oz. butter
9 oz. packet chocolate mousse

15 oz. can pear halves
A little whipped cream
Chocolate buttons

Crush biscuits or turn to crumbs using an electric blender.
Melt the butter in a saucepan, add the crushed biscuits and mix.
Press into a 7-inch flan ring on a flat serving-dish and chill.
When cold, remove flan ring.
Place mousse in centre of flan and arrange drained pear halves
  round the sides.
Decorate with whipped cream and chocolate buttons.

CHOCOLATE RIPPLE

Preparation Time: 15 minutes · Cooking Time: NIL

¼-½ pint double cream (or packet cream topping and 4 fl. oz. milk)

2 teaspoons instant coffee granules (or coffee liqueur)
3-4 serving packet instant chocolate dessert mix

Whip the cream until thick, or prepare the topping mix using the milk as directed on the packet.

Flavour with the coffee dissolved in a very little hot water (or use the liqueur alone).

Make up the chocolate instant dessert mix as directed on the packet, using ½ pint milk.

Spoon the two mixtures into sundae glasses in alternate layers.

CHRISTMAS FRITTERS

Preparation Time: 15 minutes · Cooking Time: NIL

Cold cooked Christmas pudding
1 egg

Nibbed almonds
Unsalted butter for frying
Brandy butter

Cut pudding into 2-inch squares, about ½-inch thick. Beat egg.

Dip them in beaten egg and coat with nibbed almonds.

Fry gently until pudding is heated through and almonds are golden.

Drain on absorbent paper and serve hot with leftover brandy butter.

FRUIT FINGERS

Preparation Time: 15 minutes · Cooking Time: 30 minutes

13 oz. packet frozen but thawed shortcrust pastry
1 medium-sized cooking apple
2 oz. sultanas
3 oz. stoned dates

2 oz. currants
1 oz. mixed peel
2 oz. brown sugar
1 tablespoon lemon juice
Little caster sugar

Roll out the thawed pastry on a lightly-floured board and line into a shallow square baking tin measuring 7½ inches by 7½ inches, reserving enough pastry to form a lid.

Peel, core and chop the apple. Chop the dates. Mix chopped fruit with remaining ingredients except caster sugar. Spoon into pastry case.

Cover with pastry lid, sealing edges well. Glaze with a little milk, then mark into fingers, making a small slit in each one.

Bake in a moderately hot oven, gas mark 6, 400° F., for 30 minutes or until pastry is golden.

Cool, cut into fingers and dredge with caster sugar.

Makes 12.

GINGER ALASKA

Preparation Time: 15 minutes · Cooking Time: NIL

1 ginger cake	2-3 teaspoons syrup from jar of
½ family brick vanilla ice-cream	ginger
	1 egg white
3 pieces preserved stem ginger	2 oz. caster sugar

Hollow out cake, leaving walls and base about ½ inch thick.

Slice drained stem ginger; arrange in base of hollowed cake. Spoon over ginger syrup.

Whisk egg white until stiff, add 1 teaspoon sugar and continue to whisk until very stiff; fold in remaining sugar.

Cut ice-cream to fit hollow of cake and be level with top.

Very quickly, cover top with prepared meringue mixture, making sure the ice-cream is completely covered.

Place under a very hot grill for about 2 minutes or until meringue is golden-brown.

Serve immediately.

GOOSEBERRY PUDDING

Preparation Time: 15 minutes · Cooking Time: 30 minutes

1 oz. prepared suet	2 tablespoons sugar
4 oz. brown sugar	1 pint milk
3 oz. fresh white breadcrumbs	15 oz. can gooseberries
3 tablespoons custard powder	

Combine the suet, brown sugar and breadcrumbs and mix well.
Grease a 1½ pint pie dish and line with most of this mixture.
Mix the custard powder and sugar together smoothly with a
little of the cold milk; put the rest on to heat in a saucepan.
Pour the hot milk onto the custard mixture, return to the rinsed-
out saucepan and bring to the boil, stirring all the time.
Remove from heat and add the drained gooseberries. Turn into
prepared pie dish.
Top with remaining breadcrumb mixture and bake in a hot
oven, gas mark 7, 425° F., for 30 minutes, or until top is crisp
and golden.

HOT AND COLD PUDDING

Preparation Time: 15 minutes · Cooking Time: NIL

4 slices cold, cooked Christmas pudding	½ teaspoon cinnamon
	2 tablespoons brandy
2 oz. unsalted butter	2 oz. raisins
1½ oz. caster sugar	4 small vanilla ice-cream bricks
Grated rind and juice of 1 large orange	

Cut slices of Christmas pudding, about ½-inch thick, and the
length and width of the ice-cream bricks.
Melt the butter and sauté the pudding slices until heated
through. Remove from heat and keep warm.
Add the sugar, orange rind and juice, cinnamon and the raisins
to the pan and cook quickly until sauce is slightly syrupy in
consistency.
Heat the brandy in a small saucepan, pour into the sauce and
ignite.
To serve, put a slice of Christmas pudding on each of 4 small
plates. Top with a brick of ice-cream.
Spoon the hot sauce over the ice-cream and serve at once.

KISEL

Preparation Time: 15 minutes · Cooking Time: NIL

14 oz. can raspberries
1 rounded dessertspoon cornflour

2 tablespoons sugar

Drain the raspberries, keeping the juice, and blend in a liquidiser
or rub through a sieve.

Make up the juice with water to 3/4 of a cup (3/8 pint) and mix
a little with the cornflour to make a paste.

Stir in the rest of the liquid and pour into a pan with the raspberry purée.

Bring to the boil, stirring gently.

Simmer for 1-1½ minutes, still stirring.

Pour into 3 or 4 individual glasses and chill.

Serve with 'cigarette russes' biscuits.

LEMON COCKTAIL MERINGUE

Preparation Time: 15 minutes · Cooking Time: 5-10 minutes

15 oz. can fruit cocktail
Packet lemon pie-filling
Sponge flan case

1 egg
1½ tablespoons caster sugar

Drain the fruit cocktail, reserving ¼ pint syrup from the can.

Make up the lemon pie-filling using the egg yolk, ¼ pint water
and the reserved fruit syrup, but otherwise following directions on the packet.

Stir in the drained fruit.

Place flan case on a baking sheet. Spoon the fruit mixture into
the flan.

Make a meringue from the egg white and sugar and cover top
with this mixture, making sure all the filling is coated.

Brown in a hot oven, gas mark 7, 425° F., for 5-10 minutes.

Serve hot or cold.

Delicious with vanilla ice-cream.

LEMON FRUIT SPONGE

Preparation Time: 15 minutes · Cooking Time: 35-45 minutes

1 lb. 13 oz. can diced peaches or pears	6½ oz. packet orange or lemon sponge mix
Packet lemon pie filling	Pinch salt
2 whole eggs and 1 extra yolk	Little icing sugar

Drain the fruit, reserving ½ pint of the syrup. Place fruit in a heat-proof dish.

Make up the lemon pie filling, following directions on the packet, using the egg yolk but substituting the reserved fruit syrup for the water. Spoon over the fruit.

Make up the sponge mix using the 2 whole eggs and a pinch of salt, following packet instructions. Spoon it over the fruit mixture.

Bake in a moderate oven, gas mark 5, 375° F., for 35-45 minutes or until sponge is cooked through.

Dust with icing sugar and serve hot with cream or custard.

LEMON PUDDING

Preparation Time: 15 minutes · Cooking Time: 45 minutes

2 oz. butter	2 oz. flour (self-raising or plain)
5 oz. caster sugar	Juice and rind of a lemon
2 eggs separated	½ pint milk

Cream butter and sugar, then add well-beaten egg yolks, flour, juice and rind of lemon, then milk, and, finally, the stiffly-beaten egg whites. (The mixture will be very thin.)

Put in a greased ovenproof dish and stand in an oven tin, or other large dish, containing hot water.

Bake in a moderate oven, gas mark 4, 350° F., for 45 minutes. There will be a light sponge on top and a delicious sauce underneath.

MANGO FOOL

Preparation Time: 15 minutes · Cooking Time: NIL

15½ oz. can mangoes	1½ tablespoons arrowroot
¼ pint (approx.) canned sweet-ened orange juice	1 oz. sugar
	Squeeze lemon juice
	¼ pint double cream

Drain the mangoes, reserving the syrup, and push the fruit through a sieve or make a purée in an electric blender.

Make the syrup up to ½ pint using orange juice. Blend the arrowroot with a little of the syrup and heat the remainder with the sugar in a saucepan.

When almost boiling, pour onto arrowroot mixture, stirring all the time, and return to the saucepan. Heat, stirring all the time until syrup boils and then thickens.

Mix with mango purée. Add lemon juice.

Whisk cream until lightly thickened and stir into fruit.

Chill before serving.

MOCHA CREAMS

Preparation Time: 15 minutes · Cooking Time: NIL

1 large egg	1 oz. cornflour
2 oz. margarine	½ oz. plain flour
2 oz. caster sugar	1 dessertspoon instant coffee
Small can evaporated milk	1 teaspoon cocoa
½ pint fresh milk	Grated chocolate to decorate

Place the beaten egg in a saucepan with the remaining in-gredients, except the grated chocolate.

Whisk continuously over a moderate heat, bringing the mixture to the boil.

Stir over heat for 2-3 minutes until thick and smooth.

Pour into 4 individual moulds rinsed out with cold water.

Unmould when cold and serve decorated with grated chocolate.

ORANGE MARMALADE COBBLER

Preparation Time: 15 minutes · Cooking Time: 20-25 minutes

3-4 serving packet orange-flavoured apple dessert	2 oz. butter
4 oz. self-raising flour	2 tablespoons milk
Pinch salt	3 tablespoons orange marmalade
1 tablespoon sugar	

Grease a 1½ pint ovenproof dish. Make up the apple dessert as directed on the packet and spoon into the prepared dish.

Sift the flour and salt into a bowl. Stir in the sugar.

Rub the butter in until the mixture resembles fine breadcrumbs. Mix to a soft dough with the milk.

Place on a floured board and roll out to a rectangle 6 inches by 8 inches.

Spread with the marmalade.

Roll up like a Swiss roll.

Cut into 9 slices and place, cut side up, in a circle on top of the apple dessert.

Bake in a hot oven, gas mark 7, 425° F., for 20-25 minutes until golden-brown.

Serve hot or cold with custard or cream.

ORANGE SOUFFLÉ

Preparation Time: 15 minutes · Cooking Time: 30 minutes

1½ oz. butter	7 fl. oz. milk
1½ oz. plain flour	4 oz. caster sugar
Half of 6 oz. can frozen orange juice concentrate	2 eggs

Melt the butter in a saucepan, stir in the flour and cook for 2-3 minutes.

Combine orange juice with the milk to make ½ pint of liquid. Gradually blend this mixture into the butter and flour mixture. Add the sugar.

Stir over a gentle heat until the sugar has dissolved.

Bring to boil, stirring, then simmer for 2 minutes.

Separate the eggs. Put the beaten yolks in a basin and pour the

slightly cooled sauce onto them, stirring all the time.
Beat the egg whites stiffly and fold carefully into the sauce.
Transfer to a buttered soufflé or ovenproof dish.
Cook in a moderate oven, gas mark 5, 375° F., for 30 minutes or
until soufflé has risen and is lightly set through.

PAVLOVA CAKE

Preparation Time: 15 minutes · Cooking Time: 1 hour

3 egg whites	¾ teaspoon vinegar
Pinch salt	¼ pint double cream (whipped)
6 oz. caster sugar	15 oz. can fruit salad
¾ teaspoon vanilla essence	Angelica
¾ level teaspoon cornflour	6 glacé cherries

Pre-heat oven to gas mark 3, 325° F.
Put egg whites in warm bowl with a pinch of salt and beat until
whites will stand up in peaks.
Continue beating, gradually adding sugar. The mixture should
be very stiff.
Lastly, fold in vanilla, sifted cornflour and vinegar.
Spread mixture into well-greased deep tart plate, making sides
higher than centre, and put on a low shelf in the oven.
Cook for 1 hour until crisp and brown outside and soft inside.
When cold, fill with whipped cream and place drained fruit on
top.
Decorate with cherries and angelica.
Serves 6.

PEAR AND GINGER FOOL

Preparation Time: 15 minutes · Cooking Time: NIL

1 lb. 13 oz. can pear halves	2 oz. preserved stem ginger
14½ oz. can custard	2 tablespoons ginger syrup
¼ teaspoon ground ginger	

Drain the pears. Purée them in a blender with 4 tablespoons of
the pear syrup (or push them through a sieve and then stir in
the syrup). Add the ground ginger, chopped preserved ginger
and ginger syrup.

Stir in the custard.
Serve chilled in glasses.
Serves 6.

PINEAPPLE CREAM SHELLS

Preparation Time: 15 minutes · Cooking Time: NIL

3 oz. small macaroni shells
12 oz. can pineapple pieces
Large can sweetened condensed
　milk

4 tablespoons lemon juice
Glacé cherries and angelica

Cook the macaroni shells in plenty of boiling, lightly-salted
　water until tender (about 7 minutes). Drain. Place in a 1-pint
　sized serving dish.
Drain the pineapple, reserving the juice.
Arrange pineapple over pasta and spoon a little of the juice over
　the fruit.
Pour the condensed milk into a basin and gradually stir in the
　lemon juice and 4 tablespoons of the reserved pineapple juice.
Allow 2-3 minutes for milk to thicken, then spoon it onto the
　pineapple.
Decorate with halved glacé cherries and angelica leaves.
Serve lightly chilled.

PINEAPPLE FRITTERS

Preparation Time: 15 minutes · Cooking Time: NIL

16 oz. can pineapple rings
3 oz. plain flour
Pinch salt
5-6 tablespoons tepid water

1 tablespoon oil
1 egg
Oil for deep frying
Caster sugar

Drain and dry the pineapple rings.
Sift the salt and flour into a basin. Gradually add the water and
　mix to a stiff paste.
Separate the egg. Beat egg yolk and oil into batter until smooth.
Whisk the egg white and fold in.
Coat the pineapple slices with the batter and deep fry in hot oil
　until crisp and golden.
Drain on absorbent paper and serve hot, dredged with sugar.

PRUNE AND PLUM PIE

Preparation Time: 15 minutes · Cooking Time: 25-30 minutes

15 oz. can prunes
1 lb. 3 oz. can Victoria plums

7½ oz. packet frozen but
   thawed shortcrust pastry
Little caster sugar

Drain prunes.

Drain the plums, reserving the syrup.

Place the drained fruit in a pie dish. Pour some of the plum juice over it. Do not overfill the pie dish with liquid as it will boil over when cooking.

Roll out the thawed pastry on a lightly-floured board to a rectangle slightly larger than the pie dish. Cut strips from the edges and place them round edge of dish. Brush with water.

Cover with pastry and seal edges. Trim. Make holes for steam to escape.

Brush with water and lightly springle with caster sugar.

Bake in a moderately hot oven, gas mark 6, 400° F., for 25-30 minutes or until pastry is golden.

Serve hot or cold with cream or custard.

RASPBERRY MERINGUE SPONGE

Preparation Time: 15 minutes · Cooking Time: NIL

Dairy cream sponge cake
8 oz. packet frozen raspberries
Little icing sugar

3 egg whites
4 oz. caster sugar

Remove top round of cake from thawed sponge.

Place bottom round on an ovenproof dish and arrange thawed raspberries on top of cream, pressing them in slightly.

Sprinkle with a little sifted icing sugar. Replace top sponge.

Whip the egg whites very stiffly, add 2 oz. sugar and beat again. Fold in remaining sugar.

Spread this meringue over top and sides of sponge, making sure there are no spaces. Gaps let in heat and would melt the cream.

Place in a hot oven, gas mark 7, 425° F., for 4-5 minutes, until meringue is golden-brown.

Serve immediately.

RICE WITH CHERRIES
Preparation Time: 15 minutes · Cooking Time: NIL

8 oz. can stoneless red cherries
1 tablespoon cornflour
2 oz. glacé cherries
2 oz. chopped walnuts

2 tablespoons Kirsch
15½ oz. can creamed rice
4 fl. oz. double cream

Drain cherries, reserving juice.

Blend cornflour with a little of the cherry syrup and mix with remaining syrup in a saucepan.

Bring to boil, stirring.

Soak canned cherries in 1 tablespoon Kirsch. Slice glacé cherries.

Combine creamed rice, remaining Kirsch, thickened cherry juice, glacé cherries and nuts.

Fold in whipped cream. Spoon into a serving bowl or individual glasses.

Top with whole tinned cherries.

SOUFFLÉ SURPRISE
Preparation Time: 15 minutes · Cooking Time: NIL

7-inch sponge flan case
Family brick raspberry ripple
    ice-cream (frozen hard)
15½ oz. can fruit cocktail

Packet meringue powder
3-4 tablespoons sherry
Sugar and water as shown on
    meringue packet

Set oven to gas mark 8, 450° F. Don't start to make up the dish until the correct temperature has been reached.

Put the flan case on an ovenproof plate.

Make up meringue mixture as shown on the packet.

Put the ice-cream in the centre of the flan case, shaping it with a palette knife, if necessary, to fit it in.

Spoon the drained fruit cocktail over the ice-cream, reserving a little for decoration.

Spoon the sherry over the fruit, making sure some soaks into the rim of the flan case.

Pipe or spoon the meringue over the top, sealing well to the edge of the sponge. Arrange pieces of fruit on top.

'Flash' bake near the top of the oven for 3-4 minutes till peaks are brown.
Serve immediately.

SPANISH BREAD

Preparation Time: 15 minutes · Cooking Time: NIL

4 slices stale bread, ½-inch thick
4 tablespoons milk or sweet sherry
1 egg yolk
Butter and oil for frying
Golden syrup
15 oz. can apricot halves

Trim crusts from bread. Beat milk or sherry and egg yolk together. Dip bread quickly into this mixture on both sides. Drain, then fry until crisp and golden in a mixture of butter and oil.
Heat apricots in a saucepan.
Spread syrup on one side of each piece of bread and pile the hot apricots on top. Serve at once.

SPICED BANANA PUFFS

Preparation Time: 15 minutes · Cooking Time: 20-25 minutes

7½ oz. packet frozen but thawed puff pastry
2 bananas
1 tablespoon lemon juice
1 tablespoon apricot jam
½ teaspoon ground ginger
¾ teaspoon ground nutmeg
1 oz. soft brown sugar
1 oz. raisins
A little beaten egg

Roll the thawed pastry on a lightly-floured board to an oblong 12 inches by 8 inches. Cut into six 4-inch squares.
Peel and dice the bananas and mix with lemon juice, apricot jam, spices, sugar and raisins. Place a spoonful of this mixture on the centre of each pastry square. Brush round the edges with water.
To seal, bring the 4 corners to a central point on top of mixture and seal edges very carefully.
Flute sealed edges. Brush with beaten egg to glaze.
Place puffs on a baking sheet and bake in a hot oven, gas mark 7, 425° F., for 20-25 minutes or until pastry is golden-brown and cooked through.

Serve hot or cold with cream or plain yoghurt.
Serves 6.

SPICED CRUMBLE FLAN

Preparation Time: 15 minutes · Cooking Time: 40-45 minutes

7½ oz. packet frozen but thawed shortcrust pastry
13¾ oz. can apple and black-berry pie filling
3 oz. self-raising flour

¾ teaspoon ground cinnamon
2 oz. butter
2 oz. sugar
1 tablespoon cold water

Roll out the thawed pastry on a lightly-floured board and line into a 7-inch flan ring.
Spread apple and blackberry pie filling across base of flan.
Sift flour and cinnamon into a mixing bowl. Add the sugar.
Rub in the butter until the mixture resembles fine breadcrumbs.
Add the water and mix until it is crumbly and slightly lumpy.
Sprinkle this over the pie filling, pressing down lightly.
Bake in a moderate oven, gas mark 4, 350° F., for 40-45 minutes.
Serve hot or cold.

VERA LYNN'S ORANGE DESSERT

Preparation Time: 15 minutes · Cooking Time: NIL

4 large oranges
Small can apricots
Cointreau

Flaked almonds
Honey to sweeten if wanted

Peel and slice the oranges. Purée the apricots and add a little cointreau.
Put a layer of orange slices in a dish. Sprinkle with flaked almonds.
Follow this with a layer of apricot purée, topped with flaked almonds.
Continue to layer the oranges and apricots with almonds between, finishing with almonds.
Chill until ready to serve.

20 minutes

APPLE CRACKNELL TORTE

Preparation Time: 20 minutes · Cooking Time: NIL

1 large eating apple
2 tablespoons sweet sherry
4 tablespoons water

3 oz. sugar
Frozen dairy cream sponge
cake.

Peel and core the apple and cut it into evenly-sized slices.

Place the sherry in a saucepan with the water and 1 oz. sugar. Bring to the boil, stirring until the sugar has dissolved.

Add the apple and poach gently in the syrup for about 5 minutes, keeping the slices whole. Drain, reserving the syrup.

Dissolve the remaining sugar in the liquid and boil without stirring until it is a deep caramel colour. Since the liquid is golden, do not remove from heat too early but leave until a real caramel has formed. Pour quickly onto a greased baking sheet and leave to cool.

Meanwhile, split the thawed cake in half through the cream. Arrange the apple slices on the bottom half and replace the top, cream side uppermost.

Smooth the cream on top.

Crush the caramel using the end of a rolling pin. Decorate top of cake with the pieces.

APPLE AND LIME JELLY

Preparation Time: 20 minutes · Cooking Time: NIL

1 lb. cooking apples (or 13¾ oz.
  can of apple pie filling)
Packet lime jelly

¾ pint water
¼ pint double cream

Peel, core and cook apples until tender (or use a can of apple pie filling). Blend in liquidiser until smooth.

Make up the jelly with the water. Stire in the purée.

Pour into a large dish or several small moulds.

When set, decorate with cream whipped until stiff.

APPLE MERINGUE

Preparation Time: 20 minutes · Cooking Time: 25 minutes

Two 13½ oz. cans baked apples in syrup
1 tablespoon cornflour
½ pint milk
½ teaspoon vanilla

2 eggs
1 oz. brown sugar
2 oz. glacé cherries
1 oz. angelica
4 oz. caster sugar

Drain the apples from their syrup and arrange them in an oven-proof dish.

Blend the cornflour with 2 tablespoons milk and put the rest in a saucepan to heat with the vanilla.

Separate the eggs. Mix the yolks with the cornflour mixture and stir in the brown sugar.

Chop the cherries and angelica.

Pour the hot milk onto the egg yolk and cornflour mixture. Return to the rinsed-out saucepan and stir continuously over a gentle heat until mixture thickens and reaches boiling point.

Remove from heat and stir in the glacé cherries and angelica.

Spoon over the apples.

Whisk the egg whites stiffly, add 2 teaspoons caster sugar and whisk again until very stiff. Fold in remaining sugar.

Lightly spread the meringue mixture over the apples and their sauce. Rough up top.

Bake in a moderately cool oven, gas mark 3, 325° F., for 25 minutes or until meringue is golden.

Serve hot or cold.

APRICOT TART

Preparation Time: 20 minutes · Cooking Time: NIL

7½ oz. packet frozen but thawed shortcrust pastry
7¾ oz. can apricot halves

Two 4¼ oz. cartons apricot yoghurt

Roll out the thawed pastry on a lightly-floured board and line into a 7-inch flan ring.

Prick base, line with greaseproof paper or aluminium foil and then with rice or dried beans or peas.

Bake 'blind' in a moderately hot oven, gas mark 7, 425° F., for
10 minutes. Remove paper or foil and beans or rice
Reduce oven temperature to moderate, gas mark 4, 350° F.
Drain apricots, reserving the syrup, and arrange the halves in
the flan case. Spoon the yoghurt over them.
Return to the oven and cook for a further 15 minutes.
Cool, then refrigerate.
Before serving, place the reserved apricot syrup in a small sauce-
pan and reduce over a good heat until beginning to caramelise.
Using a teaspoon, drip this syrup in a spiral across top of flan.
Serve at once.

BANANA WHIP
Preparation Time: 20 minutes · Cooking Time: NIL

4 oz. marshmallows	Juice ½ lemon
2 tablespoons milk	Packet orange jelly glaze
4 ripe (but not discoloured)	¼ pint double cream
bananas	Brown flaked almonds

Place the marshmallows and milk in a small saucepan and stir
over a gentle heat until marshmallows have dissolved.
Peel the bananas and mash well, adding the lemon juice.
Beat until smooth.
Make up the jelly glaze as directed and, when cool though not
set, add to banana purée, mixing well.
Whip the cream stiffly and fold most of it into the banana
mixture with the melted marshmallows, reserving a little
cream for decoration.
Spoon into a serving dish or individual dishes. Serve decorated
with a swirl of whipped cream and a few browned flaked
almonds.

BRANDY SNAPS
Preparation Time: 20 minutes · Cooking Time: NIL

2 oz. glacé cherries	6 oz. icing sugar
1½ oz. walnuts	Grated rind of ½ orange
2 oz. sultanas	3 dessertspoons orange juice
3 oz. butter	8-10 brandy snaps

Chop cherries, walnuts and sultanas.

Cream butter and sifted icing sugar, adding the orange juice gradually.

Beat until light and fluffy.

Stir in the grated orange rind and chopped cherries, walnuts and sultanas.

Fill mixture into a piping bag with a large, plain nozzle.

Pipe filling into both ends of the brandy snaps.

Makes 8-10.

CHEESE CAKE

Preparation Time: 20 minutes · Cooking Time: 45 minutes

7½ oz. packet frozen but
   thawed shortcrust pastry
½ lb. cream cheese
2 oz. caster sugar

2 eggs, beaten
Grated rind and juice of ½
   lemon
1 oz. sultanas

Roll the just-thawed pastry out on a lightly-floured board and line into a 7½-inch square tin. Trim.

Cream the cheese with the sugar and gradually add eggs, rind and juice. Stir in sultanas.

Pour into prepared pastry case.

Bake in a moderate oven, gas mark 4, 350° F., for about 45 minutes.

Serve cold.

Serves 6-8.

CHERRY PASTRY

Preparation Time: 20 minutes · Cooking Time: NIL

8 oz. can stoneless cherries
2-3 macaroons
7½ oz. packet frozen but
   thawed puff pastry

Oil for deep frying
2 tablespoons caster sugar

Drain the cherries and crush the macaroons.

Roll out the thawed puff pastry on a lightly-floured board until fairly thin. Cut into rounds with a cutter 3 inches in diameter and dampen edges with water.

Place 2 cherries sprinkled with crushed macaroons in the centre of each round, fold pastry over and pinch edges together to seal firmly.

Fry in hot, deep oil until golden-brown; drain well.

Serve hot, sprinkled with sugar.

CHOCOLATE CREAM

Preparation Time: 20 minutes · Cooking Time: NIL

Small can evaporated milk
½ teaspoon vanilla essence
2 teaspoons cornflour
1 teaspoon caster sugar

3 tablespoons chocolate sauce
or melted chocolate
1 egg yolk
1 oz. butter

Make the evaporated milk up to ¾ pint with water. Add the vanilla essence.

Blend the cornflour to a smooth paste with a little of the evaporated milk and heat the remainder with the sugar to boiling point.

Pour onto the cornflour, mix well and cook over gentle heat for 2-3 minutes.

Stir the chocolate sauce into the milk mixture and mix in the egg yolk. Beat well and leave to cool.

Before it is quite cool, beat in the butter.

Transfer to 4 individual glasses and chill.

CHOCOLATE NUT PANCAKES

Preparation Time: 20 minutes · Cooking Time: NIL

4½ oz. packet batter mix
1 tablespoon cocoa
2 tablespoons sugar
1 egg
2 oz. plain chocolate

2 oz. chopped hazelnuts
4 tablespoons candied honey
Grated rind ½ orange
Lard for frying
Caster or icing sugar

Empty the batter mix into a basin, sift in the cocoa and add the sugar. Make up the batter, using the egg and water, following directions on the packet.

Chop the chocolate roughly.

Toast the hazelnuts under the grill until lightly browned.

Watch them carefully because they burn very easily.

Combine hazelnuts, chocolate, honey and orange rind and mix well.

Fry the pancakes in a little lard in the usual way, turning once.

Keep them hot on an inverted plate placed over a pan of simmering water.

Spoon a little of the filling in a line across the centre of each pancake, roll them up and serve dusted with caster or icing sugar.

CHRISTMAS FLAN

Preparation Time: 20 minutes · Cooking Time: NIL

Cold cooked Christmas pudding
4 fl. oz. packet cream topping
4 fl. oz. milk
1 teaspoon gelatine

1 dessertspoon brandy or rum
2 oz. glacé cherries
Glacé or tinned pineapple to decorate

Cut pudding into thin (about ¾-inch thick) slices.

Stand an oiled 7-inch flan ring on a plate. Line base with slices of Christmas pudding, filling in any cracks with small pieces.

Make up the cream topping, using the milk and following directions on the packet.

Soften gelatine in a little cold water, then dissolve over hot water.

Chop glacé cherries and stir into cream mixture with the brandy or rum and the dissolved gelatine. Spread over the Christmas pudding and refrigerate until set.

Remove flan ring and decorate with pineapple.

COCONUT MERINGUE SLICES

Preparation Time: 20 minutes · Cooking Time: 20 minutes

13 oz. packet frozen but thawed shortcrust pastry
Raspberry jam
2 egg whites

2 oz. desiccated coconut
2 oz. caster sugar
Glacé cherries

Roll the thawed pastry on a lightly-floured board to a rectangle 9 inches by 6 inches. Line it into the base of a shallow tin of this size. Prick well and bake in a moderately hot oven, gas mark 6, 400° F., for 10-15 minutes.

Remove from oven and lower oven temperature to moderate, gas mark 4, 350° F.

Spread pastry with raspberry jam.

Whisk egg whites stiffly and fold in sugar and desiccated coconut. Spread this mixture lightly across the jam. Return to oven and bake until lightly browned (about 20 minutes).

Cut into squares and place half a glacé cherry in the centre of each one.

Serve hot or cold.

GINGER AND WALNUT CHERRY TART

Preparation Time: 20 minutes

4 oz. plain flour	1 egg yolk
2 teaspoons ground ginger	2 teaspoons water
½ teaspoon salt	15 oz. can black cherries
2 oz. butter	1 tablespoon arrowroot
1½ oz. sugar	2 teaspoons lemon juice
2 oz. finely-chopped walnuts	

Sift the flour, ginger and salt into a basin. Rub in the butter until the mixture resembles fine breadcrumbs. Add the sugar, and the chopped walnuts and mix to a soft dough with the egg yolk and water. Wrap in greaseproof paper and refrigerate for 10 minutes.

Roll out on a lightly-floured board to a round and line into a 7-inch flan ring.

Fill centre with foil or greaseproof paper and dried beans or rice. Bake 'blind' for 15 minutes in a moderate oven, gas mark 5, 375° F. Remove foil or paper and beans or rice and return to oven to dry out for a further 5-7 minutes. Cool on a wire rack.

While flan case is cooking, drain the cherries, reserving the syrup. Blend the arrowroot with a little of the cherry syrup.

Pour remaining syrup into a small saucepan, add the lemon juice and the arrowroot mixture. Bring to the boil, stirring.

Arrange the cherries in the cooled flan case. Spoon the thickened syrup over them.

Serve cold, decorated with whipped cream.

GOLDEN ORIOLE PUDDING

Preparation Time: 20 minutes · Cooking Time: NIL

13 oz. packet frozen but
thawed puff pastry
2 2½ oz. packets lemon pie
filling

2 egg yolks
¼ pint double cream
Vanilla essence
Angelica (optional)

Roll out thawed pastry thinly on a lightly-floured board and cut
into three 8-inch circles. Using a saucer, cut the centres from
two of the circles, leaving the third complete.

Place pastry rounds on dampened baking sheets and prick all
over with a fork.

Cook at gas mark 8, 450° F., for about 10 minutes or until well
risen and golden-brown. Cool on wire racks.

Meanwhile, make up lemon pie filling according to directions
on the pack, using the egg yolks and water; allow to cool.

Whip cream with a few drops of vanilla essence until stiff.

To assemble, place whole pastry base on a plate and stand the
two rings on top, spreading a little of the filling between each
and pressing gently together. Spoon remaining filling into
centre.

Decorate with whirls of whipped cream and angelica.

JAM TOP PUDDING

Preparation Time: 20 mins. · Cooking Time: 1 hour 15 mins.

Packet sponge fingers
2 eggs
Grated rind ½ lemon

¾ pint milk
Raspberry jam

Crumble the sponge fingers into a bowl.

Beat the eggs with the grated lemon rind.

Heat the milk to just below boiling point. Stir into the beaten
eggs.

Pour this mixture onto the crumbled biscuits. Stir, then leave to
stand for 10 minutes.

Grease with butter a 1½ pint basin and spread a tablespoon of
jam across the bottom.

Pour the biscuits mixture into the basin. Cover with greased greaseproof paper and a cloth; tie securely.

Steam very gently for 1-1¼ hours.

Turn out very carefully onto a heated serving-dish and serve with hot raspberry jam sauce.

MINCEMEAT CHEESECAKE

Preparation Time: 20 minutes · Cooking Time: NIL

4 oz. butter or margarine	2 tablespoons lemon juice
½ lb. digestive biscuits	1 large egg
½ teaspoon vanilla	¼ pint double cream
½ lb. cream cheese	½ lb. mincemeat
2 oz. icing sugar	1 oz. caster sugar

Melt the butter or margarine. Pound the biscuits to crumbs, or use an electric blender. Stir them into the melted butter with the vanilla.

Press this mixture onto the base and up the sides of a 9-inch pie dish or flan ring. Refrigerate while making the filling.

Cream the cheese with the icing sugar. Beat in the lemon juice and then add the beaten egg. Gradually beat in the cream.

Spread the mincemeat across the base of the biscuit crust, then spoon in the cheese mixture.

Bake in a moderate oven, gas mark 4, 350° F., for 45 minutes or until filling is set.

Sprinkle with caster sugar and place under a hot grill for 3-4 minutes until the sugar melts and forms a golden-brown caramel.

Serve cold.

PEACH FLAN

Preparation Time: 20 minutes · Cooking Time: 20-25 minutes

7½ oz. packet frozen but thawed puff pastry	2 oz. ground almonds
	15½ oz. can sliced peaches
3 tablespoons raspberry jam	1 oz. blanched almonds
1 tablespoon lemon juice	

Roll out thawed pastry thinly on a lightly-floured board.

Line into a 7-inch flan ring or sandwich tin. Trim edges, leaving ¾-inch rim.

Spread 2 tablespoons jam over pastry base, sprinkle with lemon juice and ground almonds. Arrange drained peaches on top. Turn in pastry rim and crimp with fingers.

Place half the blanched almonds on top of peaches.

Bake in a hot oven, gas mark 7, 425° F., for 20-25 minutes.

Heat remaining jam in a small saucepan with a few drops of water.

Brush peaches with this glaze and serve hot, decorated with almonds.

PEACH SPONGE CAKE

Preparation Time: 20 minutes · Cooking Time: NIL

1 block Madeira cake	4 canned peach halves
4 oz. hot sieved jam	4 tablespoons sweet wine or
2 oz. nib almonds	liqueurs
2 tablespoons cake crumbs	2 tablespoons caster sugar
2 oz. ground almonds	4 whole almonds

From the Madeira cake, cut out 4 bases, ½-inch thick, for the peach halves.

Spread with melted jam and coat with a mixture of nib almonds and cake crumbs.

Put a peach on each piece.

Blend the ground almonds with 1 tablespoon of the wine and the sugar.

Spoon this mixture (add more wine if it is too dry) into the peach halves and top with a whole almond.

Blend the remainder of the jam with the rest of the wine and pour round the peach halves.

RHUBARB FLAN

Preparation Time: 20 minutes · Cooking Time: 30-35 minutes

7½ oz. packet frozen but
  thawed shortcrust pastry
19 oz. can rhubarb
¾-1 teaspoon ground ginger
1 oz. brown sugar

3 tablespoons redcurrant jelly
1 teaspoon arrowroot
1 tablespoon water
4 oz. can cream

Roll out the thawed pastry on a lightly-floured board and line
  into a 7-inch flan ring. Drain the rhubarb.
Combine the ginger and brown sugar. Stir gently into rhubarb.
Arrange the rhubarb in the flan case, starting from the outside
  of the case.
Bake in a moderate oven, gas mark 4, 350° F., for 30-35 minutes,
  or until pastry is cooked. Remove from oven and leave to cool.
While flan is cooking, make the glaze: Melt the redcurrant
  jelly in a small saucepan. Blend the arrowroot with the water
  and add to the redcurrant jelly. Cook for 2-3 minutes, stirring
  all the time, until the glaze thickens. Cool slightly.
Spoon the glaze evenly over the rhubarb.
Serve with cream.

RUSSIAN PANCAKES WITH APRICOT

Preparation Time: 20 minutes · Cooking Time: NIL

4½ oz. packet batter mix
8 oz. packet cream cheese
1 egg
1 tablespoon icing sugar

Vanilla essence or cinnamon
Oil or lard for frying
14¼ oz. can apricot pie filling

Make up the batter using water and following the directions for
  pancakes on the packet.
Beat the softened cream cheese with the icing sugar and gradually add the beaten egg. Flavour with vanilla or cinnamon to
  taste.
Heat a very little oil or lard in a frying pan and make the pancakes in the usual way, turning them once. As each one is
  cooked, turn it out onto some kitchen paper.
When all the pancakes have been made, spread each one with a
  little cheese filling.

Fold them in half, and then in half again to form triangles.
Fry them again for 2-3 minutes in a hot pan using a little butter.
Serve with heated apricot pie filling.

SANTA'S TRIFLE

Preparation Time: 20 minutes · Cooking Time: NIL

12 oz. left-over Christmas pudding	1 tablespoon brandy or sweet sherry
Grated rind and juice of 1 orange	½ pint custard
	¼ pint double cream
	Few whole hazelnuts

Place the Christmas pudding in a bowl and break up with a fork.
Add the orange rind, juice and brandy or sherry, and mix
well.
Half fill serving glasses with Christmas pudding mixture, press-
ing it down firmly.
Pour over the custard. Allow to cool.
Decorate with piped cream and the nuts.
Serve chilled.

25 minutes

CHERRY SPLITS

Preparation Time: 25 minutes · Cooking Time: NIL

7½ oz. packet frozen but thawed puff pastry	¼ pint double cream
14¼ oz. can cherry pie filling	Icing sugar

Roll out thawed pastry on a lightly-floured board to a strip 4
inches wide and about the thickness of a 10p coin.
Cut into oblong pieces, 3 inches by 4 inches. Place on dampened
baking sheets and bake in a hot oven, gas mark 8, 450° F., for
10-15 minutes or until well-risen and golden.
Cool on a wire rack.
Whisk cream until stiff.
Split the pastry slices horizontally. Spread base with pie filling

and top with whipped cream. Cover with top half of pastry. Dust with sifted icing sugar.

Makes about 9.

CHERRY, STRAWBERRY AND MANDARIN TRIFLE

Preparation Time: 25 minutes · Cooking Time: NIL

½ lb. frozen strawberries	3 tablespoons redcurrant jelly
2 oz. caster sugar	¼ pint double cream
2 individual trifle sponges	Little icing sugar
10 oz. can stoned cherries	11 oz. can mandarin oranges
2½ fl. oz. red wine	

Sprinkle the strawberries with 1 oz. caster sugar and leave to thaw.

Cut the trifle sponges in half horizontally.

Put one in the base of each of 4 individual ramekin or similar dishes, trimming the sponges to fit, if necessary.

Drain the cherries, reserving the syrup, and arrange on top of the sponges.

Measure 2½ fl. oz. of the cherry syrup into a saucepan with the wine and the remaining sugar.

Stir over a gentle heat until the sugar has dissolved. Bring to the boil.

Add the redcurrant jelly, and simmer gently until it has melted.

Remove from heat and cool slightly before pouring over the sponges.

Whip the cream until lightly stiffened.

Fold in the thawed and halved strawberries.

If you want a sweeter mixture, add a little sifted icing sugar until you get the sweetness you want.

Spoon cream and strawberry mixture over the cherries.

Drain the mandarins and arrange some segments around the top of each trifle.

Serve chilled.

CHOCOLATE STEP CAKE

Preparation Time: 25 minutes · Cooking Time: NIL

4 oz. unsalted butter
4 oz. icing sugar
4 egg yolks
4 oz. plain chocolate, melted
A little rum

2 tablespoons strong black
coffee
1 oz. sugar
24 sponge finger biscuits
Chopped walnuts

Cream butter and sifted icing sugar until light and fluffy.
Gradually add the beaten egg yolks, then the melted chocolate.
Flavour with rum.
Place sugar and coffee in a small saucepan and bring to the boil,
stirring until the sugar has dissolved. Add 1 tablespoon rum.
Spoon the rum syrup over the sponge finger biscuits.
Place 4 sponge fingers side by side on a serving-dish with 4 more
lined up end to end behind them. Spread with chocolate
cream.
Top with 8 more sponge fingers, a further layer of the cream
and finally the remaining fingers. Spread the top and sides
with the remaining chocolate cream. Rough up.
Chill for several hours.
Decorate, before serving, with chopped walnuts.

LEMON CREAM PANCAKES

Preparation Time: 25 minutes · Cooking Time: NIL

7 oz. packet batter mix
2 tablespoons melted butter
1 tablespoon caster sugar
Packet lemon pie filling

1 egg yolk
Oil for frying
Icing sugar

Make up batter according to instructions on packet, adding the
melted butter and caster sugar.
Make up lemon pie filling with egg yolk and water, following
packet directions.
Heat oil in a frying-pan and cook pancakes in the usual way,
turning once.
Keep them warm until all have been cooked.
Place a little pie filling down the centre of each pancake and roll
up.
Serve immediately, dusted with sifted icing sugar.

LEMON CHOCOLATE PIE

Preparation Time: 25 minutes · Cooking Time: NIL

4 oz. digestive biscuits
1 tablespoon sugar
2 oz. butter
Small can sweetened condensed
   milk

4 oz. can cream
1 lemon
2 squares milk chocolate

To make the pie case: break the digestive biscuits and turn to
  crumbs in an electric blender. Alternatively, place the roughly
  broken biscuits in a plastic bag and secure opening with an
  elastic band. Crush with the end of a rolling-pin.
Add the sugar.
Melt the butter and mix with the crumbs to bind them together.
Use this mixture to line the base and sides of a 7-inch flan ring
  or sandwich tin, pressing it firmly in place. Chill until set.
Meanwhile, prepare the filling: Blend together the condensed
  milk and cream. Grate the rind from the lemon, then extract
  the juice. Stir into milk mixture. This will thicken it.
Pour into prepared biscuit case and top with grated chocolate.

LEMON FLAN

Preparation Time: 25 minutes · Cooking Time: NIL

5 oz. plain sweet biscuits
1 oz. brown sugar
2 oz. butter, melted
11 fl. oz. carton lemon mousse

2 tablespoons caster sugar
¼ pint double cream
Grated rind and juice of 1
  lemon

Crush the biscuits.
Stir in the melted butter and brown sugar.
Press into a shallow 7-inch flan tin.
Leave to set.
Meanwhile, cream the lemon mousse with a fork.
Add lemon rind, juice and caster sugar, and mix well.
Whip cream until thick and fold into the lemon mixture. Pour
  into biscuit case.
Decorate with whipped cream.

LEMON PIE

Preparation Time: 25 minutes · Cooking Time: NIL

4 oz. wholemeal biscuits	2 standard eggs
4 oz. soft brown sugar	4 oz. caster sugar
1 teaspoon cinnamon	Grated rind and juice of 2
¼ teaspoon ground ginger	large lemons
¼ teaspoon ground cloves	Large can evaporated milk
½ teaspoon ground nutmeg	Lemon jelly slices
3 oz. butter or margarine	

To make the spiced crumb case, make the biscuits into crumbs
using a blender or by placing the biscuits in a plastic bag and
crushing with the end of a rolling-pin.

Place the crumbs in a bowl with the spices and brown sugar.

Melt the butter or margarine and combine with the crumb
mixture.

Line base and sides of an oblong tin, 11 inches by 7 inches, with
2 strips of aluminium foil, one covering the length of the tin
and the other the width. Leave extra length to make removal
of finished pie easier.

Cover the base of the prepared tin with the crumb crust, pressing it into place, and continuing the mixture up the sides of
the tin.

Chill till set.

Beat egg yolks with caster sugar, stir in lemon rind and juice.

Whisk egg whites until stiff and chilled evaporated milk until
very thick.

Fold into lemon mixture. Spoon into prepared crumb case.

Chill until set.

Decorate with lemon jelly slices and serve cold.

STRAWBERRY TARTS

Preparation Time: 25 minutes · Cooking Time: NIL

½ lb. packet frozen straw-	4 fl. oz. packet cream topping
berries	4 fl. oz. milk
Little caster sugar	Grated rind ½ orange
7½ oz. packet frozen but	4 oz. redcurrant jelly
thawed shortcrust pastry	

Sprinkle the strawberries with a little caster sugar and leave to thaw.

Roll out the thawed pastry on a lightly-floured board.

Cut out 4 rounds about 4½ inches in diameter and line into individual Yorkshire pudding tins. Prick bases, line with aluminium foil or greaseproof paper and weight down with dried beans or rice. Bake in a hot oven, gas mark 7, 425° F., for 10 minutes.

Remove foil or paper and rice or beans. Return to oven for a few minutes to dry out. Remove and cool.

Meanwhile, make up the creamy topping, using the milk, and following directions on packet. Stir in grated orange rind.

Divide mixture between the 4 pastry cases and spread across bases. Arrange thawed strawberries on top.

Melt the redcurrant jelly with a very little water over a gentle heat.

When smooth, spoon this glaze over the strawberries.

Cakes/Biscuits/Confectionery

Cakes/Biscuits/Confectionery
5 minutes

FLAPJACKS

Preparation Time: 5 minutes · Cooking Time: 25-30 minutes

6 oz. butter or margarine
6 oz. demerara sugar

8 oz. rolled oats
Pinch salt

Melt the butter in a saucepan over a very gentle heat.
Stir in the sugar, oats and salt and mix thoroughly.
Turn into a greased shallow Swiss roll tin and press together.
Smooth surface with a knife.
Bake in a moderately hot oven, gas mark 5, 375° F., for 25-30
    minutes.
Remove from oven and leave for a few minutes.
Cut into 16 squares or fingers and leave in tin until quite cold.

10 minutes

APPLE BUNS

Preparation Time: 10 minutes · Cooking Time: 20-25 minutes

6 oz. sachet scone mix
1 egg
2 tablespoons water

6-8 oz. peeled and chopped
    apples (about 2 eating apples)

Empty packet of scone mix into a bowl. Add chopped apples
    and mix well. Add egg and water and mix to a soft consist-
    ency.
Place a dessertspoon of the mixture into greased deep bun tins.
Bake in a moderate oven, gas mark 5, 375° F., for 20-25 minutes.
Remove from tins while still hot, make a slit at the top of each
    bun and place a knob of butter in the slit.
Serve hot.

BANANA FRUIT LOAF

Preparation Time: 10 mins. · Cooking Time: 1 hour 30 mins.

8 oz. self-raising flour
½ teaspoon salt
½ teaspoon mixed spice
4 oz. softened butter
4 oz. caster sugar
1 tablespoon clear honey

4 oz. sultanas
2 oz. glacé cherries (optional)
2 oz. chopped walnuts
1 lb. ripe bananas
2 eggs

Grease a 2 lb. loaf tin.

Sift flour, salt and spice into a bowl. Add the butter, cut into small pieces, and the quartered cherries (if used).

Peel and mash the bananas and add to the bowl with the remaining ingredients.

Beat well with a wooden spoon until mixture is well blended and smooth. Turn into prepared tin.

Bake in the centre of a moderate oven, gas mark 4, 350° F., for 1 hour, then reduce heat to moderately slow, gas mark 3, 325° F., for a further 15-30 minutes, or until a skewer inserted in the centre comes out clean. Cool on a wire rack.

This loaf has a nice, sticky consistency. Serve it sliced and buttered.

CARAMEL FINGERS

Preparation Time: 10 minutes · Cooking Time: NIL

2 tablespoons honey
2 tablespoons brown sugar

4 oz. chopped walnuts
4 tablespoons rolled oats

Place honey and brown sugar in a saucepan and stir over a gentle heat until sugar has dissolved.

Bring to boil and cook until mixture begins to caramelise—about 2-3 minutes.

Remove from heat and stir in nuts and oats.

Pour mixture onto a dampened baking sheet and shape into a rectangle about ¼ inch thick, using a wet rolling-pin.

While still hot, cut into fingers.

Leave to cool.

Makes 10-12.

CHOCOLATE ICING

Preparation Time: 10 minutes · Cooking Time: NIL

1 tablespoon cocoa
1 oz. butter
2 fl. oz. milk
1½ oz. brown sugar

1 teaspoon coffee essence
Pinch salt
Approx. 4½ oz. icing sugar

Place all ingredients, except the icing sugar, in a saucepan.

Bring to the boil, stirring until the sugar has dissolved.

Remove from heat and allow to cool slightly.

Add enough sifted icing sugar to give a thick pouring consistency.

Stand the cake to be iced on a wire rack placed over a large bowl.

Pour the icing over top of cake and allow to flow down the sides.

COCONUT BISCUITS

Preparation Time: 10 minutes · Cooking Time: 10-15 minutes

2 oz. desiccated coconut
2 oz. rolled oats
2 oz. plain flour
3 oz. soft brown sugar

3 oz. butter
1 tablespoon golden syrup
½ teaspoon bicarbonate of soda
1 teaspoon hot water

Mix together the coconut, oats, sifted flour and sugar.

Place the butter and syrup in a small saucepan and heat gently until butter has melted.

Dissolve the bicarbonate of soda in the hot water and add to the melted butter mixture.

Pour onto the dry ingredients, mix well and put half a teaspoon of the mixture onto well-greased baking sheets (spaced well apart as the mixture spreads).

Bake in a moderate oven, gas mark 5, 375° F., for 10-15 minutes, or until a rich golden-brown.

Remove from oven and leave the biscuits on the baking sheets for about 30 seconds before lifting off carefully with a flat knife onto a wire tray to cool.

COCONUT PYRAMIDS

Preparation Time: 10 minutes · Cooking Time: 10-15 minutes

Small can sweetened condensed
  milk
8 oz. desiccated coconut

1 teaspoon vanilla
Food colourings

Combine first three ingredients and mix well.
Divide the mixture into four equal portions: leave one plain,
  colour one pink, the third pale green and the fourth blue.
Shape into cones on rice paper or a greased baking-sheet.
Bake in a moderately cool oven, gas mark 3, 325° F., for 10-15
  minutes. Cool on wire rack.
Makes about 18 pyramids.

COFFEE CAKE

Preparation Time: 10 minutes · Cooking Time: 25 minutes

4 oz. self-raising flour
2 tablespoons instant coffee
  powder
2 oz. caster sugar

2 oz. butter or margarine
4 oz. golden syrup
1 egg
2 tablespoons milk

Grease an 8-inch sandwich tin and line the bottom with a round
  of greased greaseproof paper.
Stir flour and coffee into a bowl.
Melt butter or margarine, syrup, and sugar together over gentle
  heat, and cool a little.
Beat egg and milk, combine with syrup mixture, pour into dry
  ingredients and beat until smooth.
Bake in a moderate oven, gas mark 5, 375° F., for 25 minutes.
Turn onto wire cooling rack.
This cake can be iced with coffee icing when cool.

COFFEE FUDGE

Preparation Time: 10 minutes · Cooking Time: NIL

2 tablespoons instant coffee
4 oz. plain chocolate
3 tablespoons evaporated milk

2 oz. butter
1 lb. icing sugar

Dissolve the coffee in about a tablespoon of hot water.

Place in a bowl with the chocolate, broken into small pieces, and butter, and stand in a saucepan containing hot water.

Heat gently until chocolate and butter have melted. Remove from heat and stir until smooth.

Add milk and slowly work in the sieved icing sugar.

Pour into a tin and leave to set.

Cut into small squares.

For a special occasion, use small, shaped cutters.

CUP CAKES

Preparation Time: 10 minutes · Cooking Time: 15 minutes

6 oz. self-raising flour	4 tablespoons milk
¼ teaspoon salt	Little vanilla
5 oz. caster sugar	*Glacé icing*: ½-¾ lb. icing
3½ oz. white cooking fat	sugar
2 eggs	

Line 18 patty tins with paper cases.

Sift flour and salt into a mixing bowl. Add the remaining ingredients except icing sugar.

Beat with wooden spoon (or electric mixer) for 1-2 minutes till smooth and creamy.

Divide between the patty tins.

Bake at gas mark 6, 400° F., for 15 minutes.

Cool.

Ice.

To make the icing, sift ½-¾ lb. icing sugar into a basin, add sufficient cold water to give a good coating consistency and beat until smooth.

If the flavouring to be added is in liquid form, add this to the icing sugar before mixing it with water, as the addition of water may make the icing too runny.

CUP CAKE VARIATIONS

Preparation Time: 10 minutes · Cooking Time: 15 minutes

Cherry

Stir 2 oz. chopped glacé cherries into the cake mixture.
Ice with plain glacé icing and decorate with half a glacé cherry.

Chocolate

Replace 2 tablespoons flour with 2 tablespoons cocoa, sifted with
the flour and salt.
Ice with chocolate-flavoured glacé icing and decorate with halved
chocolate buttons.

Chocolate Chip

Add 2 oz. chocolate dots to the cake mixture.
Ice with plain glacé icing and decorate with a chocolate dot.

Coconut

Stir 1 oz. desiccated coconut into cake mixture.
Ice with plain glacé icing and sprinkle, while icing is still soft,
with toasted or plain desiccated coconut.

Coffee

Use 1 tablespoon coffee and chicory essence or 1 tablespoon
strong coffee and use only 3 tablespoons milk.
Omit vanilla.
Ice with coffee-flavoured glacé icing.

Dried Fruit

Add 2 oz. currants or sultanas, or a mixture of both, to the cake
mixture.
Ice with plain glacé icing and decorate with a currant or a
sultana.

Ginger

Make cake, adding 1 teaspoon ground ginger and omitting
vanilla.
Add a little finely chopped stem or crystallised ginger, if liked.
 Ice with glacé icing made with a little syrup from a jar of

stem ginger. Decorate with a small slice of stem or crystallised ginger.

Hazelnut
Stir 1½ oz. ground hazelnuts into the cake mixture in place of 1½ oz. flour.
Ice with plain glacé icing and decorate with a whole hazelnut kernel.

Lemon
Make cake as for orange cup cakes, using lemon rind in place of orange rind.
Make glacé icing with lemon juice in place of the water, and colour pale yellow with food colouring.
Decorate with a lemon sweet resembling a lemon slice.

Mixed Peel
Stir 2 oz. chopped mixed peel into the cake mixture.
Ice with plain glacé icing and decorate each cake with a few small pieces of mixed peel.

Orange
Flavour the cake mixture with grated orange rind.
Omit vanilla.
Make glacé icing, using a little orange juice in place of water, and colour orange with food colourings.
Decorate with a jelly sweet resembling an orange slice.

Walnut
Add 1 oz. chopped walnuts to the cake mixture.
Ice with plain glacé icing and decorate with a walnut half.

DEVON SPICED FRUIT CAKE

Preparation Time: 10 minutes · Cooking Time: 25-30 minutes

1 oz. sultanas
1 oz. raisins
1 oz. chopped walnuts
1 teaspoon mixed spice

1 packet Devon sponge sandwich cake mix
1 egg

Well grease a 7-inch cake tin and dust out with flour.

Chop sultanas and raisins finely.

Add mixed spice to contents of sponge mix.

Make up sponge following directions on the packet, using the egg and water. Fold in chopped fruit and the walnuts.

Pour into prepared cake tin and bake in a moderately hot oven, gas mark 6, 400° F., for 25-30 minutes.

Turn onto a wire rack to cool.

GINGERBREAD

Preparation Time: 10 mins. · Cooking Time: 1 hour 5 mins.

8 oz. self-raising flour
Pinch salt
2 heaped teaspoons ground
ginger
1 teaspoon ground cinnamon
4 oz. suet
4 oz. soft brown sugar

1 oz. preserved stem ginger
1 oz. chopped walnuts
2 beaten eggs
4-6 tablespoons milk
6 tablespoons black treacle or
golden syrup
2 teaspoons granulated sugar

Sift the flour, salt and spices into a mixing bowl.

Add the suet, brown sugar, chopped preserved ginger and walnuts, mix thoroughly.

Heat the treacle or syrup gently and stir in the milk.

Remove from heat and add beaten eggs. Stir into dry ingredients making sure mixture is smooth.

Pour into a greased, lined 7-inch cake tin.

Sprinkle with granulated sugar, cover tin with greaseproof paper and bake in the centre of a moderate oven, gas mark 4, 350° F., for 1 hour.

Leave in tin for 5 minutes after removing from oven; turn onto wire rack. Cool.

This gingerbread improves if kept for 2-3 days.

GINGER CAKE
Preparation Time: 10 minutes · Cooking Time: 40-45 minutes

9 oz. plain flour
Pinch salt
7 oz. unsalted butter

7 oz. caster sugar
3 oz. preserved ginger
1 egg

Sift flour and salt into a mixing bowl. Add the butter, cut into small pieces, and the sugar. Drain the ginger from its syrup and chop finely. Beat the egg.

Add the ginger and most of the egg (reserving a little for glazing) to the flour mixture. Knead all ingredients together to form a smooth dough.

Press into an 8-inch cake tin, smoothing the top, and brush with the reserved beaten egg.

Using a fork, mark a border round the edge and a lattice design across the centre.

Bake in a moderate oven, gas mark 4, 350° F., for 40-45 minutes or until golden brown. Turn out onto a wire rack to cool. Serve cut into slices.

ICED CHOCOLATE CHERRY CAKE
Preparation Time: 10 minutes · Cooking Time 1 hour

4 oz. whipped-up fat
4 oz. caster sugar
3 standard eggs
4 tablespoons milk
6 oz. self-raising flour
1 oz. cocoa
¼ teaspoon salt

6 oz. mixed fried fruit
2 oz. glacé cherries
1 oz. angelica
1 oz. walnut pieces
½ lb. icing sugar
Few extra glacé cherries
Walnut halves

Cut up the fat and place in a mixing bowl with the sugar, 2 eggs plus the yolk of a third, and the milk. Sift in the flour, cocoa and salt. Beat well for 1 minute.

Fold in the mixed dried fruit, halved glacé cherries, chopped angelica and the walnut pieces.

Turn into a greased 7-inch cake tin with a round of greased greaseproof paper in the base.

Bake in a moderate oven, gasmark 4, 350° F., for about 1 hour, or when a skewer inserted in the centre comes out clean. Turn onto a wire rack to cool.

When cake is cold prepare the icing. Beat the icing sugar with the remaining egg white until the mixture will stand in peaks.

Spread over the cake. Decorate with extra cherries and halved walnuts.

MALTED LOAF

Preparation Time: 10 minutes · Cooking Time: 1 hour

½ lb. self-raising flour
2 oz. chocolate malt beverage granules
2 oz. sugar
3 oz. mixed dried fruit

1 oz. chopped dates
2 tablespoons warmed golden syrup
¼ pint (approximately) milk and water

Sift the flour into a mixing bowl and add the remaining dry ingredients and the fruit.

Stir in the warmed syrup and mix to a dropping consistency with the liquid.

Pour into a greased 1 lb. loaf tin and bake in a moderate oven, gas mark 4, 350° F., for about 1 hour.

Turn out and cool on a wire rack.

This loaf improves by storing in an airtight tin for a day before serving.

Slice thinly and spread with butter.

NO-BAKE OAT FINGERS

Preparation Time: 10 minutes · Cooking Time: NIL

4 oz. sugar
4 oz. butter
1 tablespoon water
7 oz. instant porridge oats

1 oz. desiccated coconut
1 dessertspoon instant coffee, or cocoa

Put sugar, butter and water in a pan and bring to the boil slowly.

Remove from heat and mix with the dry ingredients in a bowl.

Put in a light-greased toffee-tin and allow to become firm.

When nearly set, cut into fingers.

PINEAPPLE CAKE

Preparation Time: 10 minutes · Cooking Time: 20 minutes

7 oz. self-raising flour
5 oz. caster sugar
3 oz. butter
4 oz. chopped canned pine-
    apple
2 eggs

¼ teaspoon salt
5 oz. well-drained chopped
    pineapple
5-8 oz. icing sugar
2 teaspoons lemon juice

Put the flour and sugar in mixing bowl.
Put butter, pineapple, eggs and salt in blender until smooth.
Combine with dry ingredients.
Pour into two 6½-inch greased sandwich tins.
Bake at gas mark, 5, 375° F., for 20 minutes.
When cooked, cool on a rack.
Make filling by blending pineapple, icing sugar and lemon juice,
    and spread between cakes.
The top of the cake may be iced and decorated if liked.
(You can sprinkle icing sugar over, or ice it with glacé icing
    made with 8 oz. of icing sugar, 1 teaspoon lemon juice, and
    about 3 tablespoons pineapple juice.)

PINEAPPLE UPSIDE-DOWN CAKE

Preparation Time: 10 minutes · Cooking Time: 45 minutes

16 oz. can pineapple rings
Glacé cherries
5 oz. packet multi-mix sponge
1½ oz. sugar

1 egg
2½ tablespoons milk
2 oz. Demerara sugar

Grease a 7-inch cake tin. Sprinkle base with Demerara sugar.
Drain the juice from the pineapple rings and arrange rings on
    sugar, placing a glacé cherry in the centre of each ring.
Make up sponge mix according to the directions on the packet
    using the sugar, egg and milk.
Carefully spoon over the fruit.
Bake in a moderately cool oven, gas mark 3, 325° F., for 45
    minutes before turning out onto a wire rack to cool.

QUICK CHOCOLATE CAKE

Preparation Time: 10 minutes · Cooking Time: 1 hour

4 oz. butter	6 fl. oz. milk
½ lb. self-raising flour	2 eggs
3 tablespoons cocoa	½ teaspoon vanilla
6 oz. sugar	

Melt the butter in a saucepan. Allow to cool.

Place remaining ingredients in a bowl. Pour in the cooled butter and beat well for 3 minutes.

Turn into a well-greased 7-inch cake tin, with a round of greased greaseproof paper in the base.

Bake in a moderate oven, gas mark 4, 350° F., for about 1 hour, or until cake is done when tested.

Remove from oven and leave for a few minutes in the tin before turning out onto a wire rack to cool.

When cold, ice with chocolate icing.

Chocolate caraque, used as a decoration, looks pretty but takes a little time. Melt 1 oz. plain chocolate in a bowl over hot water; then stir until smooth, spread thinly on a flat cold surface (preferably marble) and leave until barely set.

Using a sharp knife, curl off the chocolate.

RAISIN CRUNCHIES

Preparation Time: 10 minutes · Cooking Time: NIL

4 oz. packet chocolate dots	2 oz. nut brittle
Few drops vanilla	1 oz. cornflakes
¼ lb. seedless raisins	

Place the chocolate dots in a basin standing in a saucepan of hot water and heat until melted, stirring until smooth. Remove from heat.

Meanwhile, break the nut brittle into small pieces, crushing it with the end of a rolling pin, if necessary.

Crush the cornflakes slightly.

Add raisins, brittle, cornflakes and vanilla to melted chocolate and stir until well coated.

Drop in small mounds onto waxed paper or into paper sweet-cases from a teaspoon.

Chill until set.
Makes approximately 16.

SPICED APPLE CAKE
Preparation Time: 10 minutes · Cooking Time: 35 minutes

5 oz. packet multi-mix sponge	1 oz. chopped walnuts
1½ oz. sugar	1 teaspoon ground cinnamon
1 egg	1 tablespoon caster sugar
2½ tablespoons milk	2-3 tablespoons apple sauce

Grease a 6½-inch cake tin with lard or butter.
Make up sponge mixture according to directions on the pack, using sugar, egg and milk.
Combine chopped walnuts, cinnamon and caster sugar.
Spoon half the cake mixture into the base of the prepared cake tin.
Cover with apple sauce and half the nut mixture.
Spoon over remaining sponge mixture.
Sprinkle top with remaining nut mixture.
Bake in a moderately hot oven, gas mark 5, 375° F., for 30 minutes.
Remove from oven, allow to cool for 5 minutes then turn out of tin.
Cool on a wire rack.

15 minutes

CHOCOLATE HAZELNUT TRUFFLES
Preparation Time: 15 minutes · Cooking Time: NIL

4 oz. Madeira cake	1-2 teaspoons milk
4 tablespoons chocolate hazel-nut spread	1 oz. shelled hazelnuts
1 dessertspoon rum	1 oz. chopped hazelnuts

Make the cake into crumbs by sieving or using an electric blender.

Mix cake crumbs with chocolate hazelnut spread and the rum.
Add enough milk to bind.

Taking a little of this mixture and one hazelnut, form into a
small ball with the nut in the centre.

Repeat with remaining nuts and mixture.

Roll balls in chopped hazelnuts.

CHOCOLATE ORANGE TRUFFLES

Preparation Time: 15 minutes · Cooking Time: NIL

4 oz. Madeira cake
2-3 tablespoons chocolate
spread
Grated rind of ½ orange

A little orange juice or orange
liqueur
Chocolate vermicelli

Make the cake into crumbs by sieving or using an electric
blender.

Mix cake crumbs with chocolate spread and grated orange rind.
Add enough orange juice or orange liqueur to bind.

Form mixture into small balls the size of a walnut.

Roll each one in chocolate vermicelli.

Makes about 12.

CHOCOLATE WALNUT FUDGE

Preparation Time: 15 minutes · Cooking Time: NIL

¼ lb. marshmallows
Small can evaporated milk
¾ lb. sugar
Pinch salt

2 oz. butter
6 oz. chocolate dots
1 teaspoon vanilla
4 oz. chopped walnuts

Combine marshmallows, milk, sugar, salt and butter in a saucepan. Stir over a gentle heat until marshmallows, sugar and
butter have melted. Bring to the boil and boil for 5 minutes.
Remove from heat.

Meanwhile, dissolve the chocolate dots in a basin over a pan of
hot water. Stir into marshmallows mixture with the vanilla
and walnuts. Pour into a greased 7-inch square tin.

Cool until firm. Cut into small squares.

COCONUT ICE

Preparation Time: 15 minutes · Cooking Time: NIL

Large can sweetened condensed
   milk
12 oz. icing sugar

6 oz. desiccated coconut
Red food colouring

Mix together the condensed milk and sifted icing sugar.
Stir in the coconut (the mixture should be very stiff) and divide
   into 2 parts.
Tint one half of the mixture pale pink with a few drops of red
   colouring.
Spread one mixture in the base of an oiled square or round cake
   tin.
Top with remaining mixture.
Refrigerate overnight.
When set, cut into squares. Store in refrigerator.

COCONUT RUMBAS

Preparation Time: 15 minutes · Cooking Time: NIL

4 oz. margarine
4 oz. soft brown sugar
1 tablespoon cocoa
1 tablespoon milk
2 tablespoons rum or sherry

2 small teacups rolled oats
2 small teacups desiccated
   coconut
Extra desiccated coconut or
   chocolate vermicelli

Melt margarine and sugar in a saucepan over low heat.
Add milk and cocoa and bring to the boil. Boil gently for 2
   minutes.
Remove from heat, stir in rum or sherry and then the oats and
   coconut. Mix well. Form into small balls and roll in coconut
   or chocolate vermicelli.
Set overnight.

CRUMBLE CAKE

Preparation Time: 15 minutes · Cooking Time: NIL

7½ oz. packet plain sweet
    biscuits
2 oz. butter or margarine

1 oz. sugar
1 tablespoon golden syrup
1 tablespoon cocoa

Break the biscuits into small pieces.

Melt the butter or margarine, sugar and syrup in a saucepan
over a gentle heat, but do not boil. Add the cocoa and mix
well.

Stir in the crushed biscuits.

Press the mixture into a greased, loose-bottomed 6-inch cake tin
and leave overnight.

To serve: turn out and cut into small slices.

DANISH CHOCOLATE CAKE

Preparation Time: 15 minutes · Cooking Time: NIL

8 oz. butter
8 oz. plain chocolate
2 eggs
2 level tablespoons sugar

8 oz. crushed shortcake biscuits
8 oz. glacé cherries
2 oz. walnuts

Melt butter and chocolate in a pan over hot water.

Beat the eggs, mix in sugar and chocolate mixture, and stir until
well blended.

Mix in crushed biscuits, chopped cherries and nuts.

Smooth mixture into a greased and lined cake tin and leave to
set.

DIVINITY DROPS

Preparation Time: 15 minutes · Cooking Time: 20 minutes

2 oz. cornflakes
3 oz. stoned dates
1 oz. chopped walnuts
1 oz. nibbed almonds
1½ oz. desiccated coconut
2 egg whites

Pinch salt
½ teaspoon cream of tartar
¼ teaspoon almond essence
½ teaspoon vanilla essence
3 oz. soft brown sugar

Crush the cornflakes finely. Chop the dates. Combine cornflakes, dates, walnuts, almonds and coconut and mix well.

Whisk egg whites until frothy. Add salt, cream of tartar and the essences. Continue whisking until soft peaks form.

Add the brown sugar gradually, whisking until stiff but not dry. Fold in cornflake mixture.

Drop level tablespoonsful, 2 inches apart, onto greased baking trays or onto rice paper placed on baking trays.

Bake in a moderately slow oven, gas mark 3, 325° F., for about 20 minutes or until set and lightly browned. Cool on a wire rack. Makes about 20.

ECCLES CAKES

Preparation Time: 15 minutes · Cooking Time: 15 minutes

2 oz. butter	Little lemon juice
2 oz. brown sugar	Pinch mixed spice
4 oz. currants	13 oz. packet frozen but
2 oz. cut mixed peel	thawed puff pastry

Melt the butter in a saucepan. Add brown sugar, currants, mixed peel, mixed spice and lemon juice to taste. Remove from heat and leave to cool slightly.

Roll out the thawed pastry on a lightly-floured board to the thickness of a penny. Cut out rounds using a 4-inch plain pastry cutter.

Place a heaped teaspoon of the filling onto the centre of each round. Brush edges with water.

Fold pastry to centre, sealing carefully. Turn Eccles cakes over and press out slightly. Brush with water and sprinkle with sugar. Place on a baking-sheet.

Bake in a hot oven, gas mark 7, 425° F., for 15 minutes.

Cool on a wire rack and serve warm or cold.

GRIDDLE CAKES

Preparation Time: 15 minutes · Cooking Time: NIL

5 oz. plain flour	1 egg
3 teaspoons baking powder	2 oz. golden syrup
1 oz. melted margarine	¼ pint milk

Sift flour and baking powder into a bowl. Make a well in the centre.

Add the syrup, egg and margarine, then enough milk to mix smoothly. Beat in the rest of the milk to form a thick batter. Beat until smooth.

Rub a griddle, hot plate or frying pan lightly with lard.

Drop dessertspoonsful of the mixture onto the hot surface and cook until golden; turn and brown second side.

Cover with a cloth while cooling.

Serve buttered with more golden syrup.

HONEY BREAD

Preparation Time: 15 mins. · Cooking Time: 1 hour 5 mins.

8 oz. honey	½ teaspoon ground mace
2 tablespoons oil	3 eggs
1 lb. plain flour	4 oz. chopped candied peel
1 teaspoon bicarbonate soda	Grate rind ½ lemon
1 teaspoon ground ginger	8 oz. sugar
1 teaspoon cinnamon	2 oz. flaked almonds

Place the honey and oil in a saucepan and warm gently until combined. Remove from heat.

Sift dry ingredients (including spices) into a bowl.

Make a hollow in the centre and pour in the beaten eggs, candied peel, lemon rind and sugar, and lastly the honey mixture.

Mix to a smooth batter. Turn mixture into a greased shallow tin (about 11 inches by 7 inches). Sprinkle with flaked almonds.

Bake in a moderate oven, gas mark 4, 350° F., for 1 hour.

Cool tin for 5 minutes, then turn onto a wire rack and leave until quite cold.

To serve, cut into slices and spread with butter.

JANHAGEL

Preparation Time: 15 minutes · Cooking Time: 20-25 minutes

6 oz. plain flour	4 oz. butter
½ teaspoon cinnamon	1 tablespoon granulated sugar
2 oz. caster sugar	1 oz. flaked almonds

Sift the flour and cinnamon into a bowl and add the caster sugar. Rub in the butter. Work mixture together.

Press into a buttered swiss roll tin and flatten surface.

Sprinkle with granulated sugar and flaked almonds. Press nuts in slightly.

Bake in a moderate oven, gas mark 4, 350° F., for 20-25 minutes until golden-brown.

Cut into fingers while still warm and cool on a cooling rack.

Makes 18 biscuits, which keep well in an airtight tin.

MARBLE CAKE

Preparation Time: 15 minutes · Cooking Time: 25-30 minutes

6¾ oz. packet Madeira cake mix	1 dessertspoon cocoa
1 egg	Cochineal

Grease and lightly flour a 6-inch round cake tin.

Make up the cake following directions on packet, using the egg and 4 tablespoons water.

Divide the mixture into 3 equal parts. Colour one-third with a little cochineal. To the second add the sieved cocoa and a very little warm water. Keep the remaining third plain.

Using a spoon, drop alternate spoonfuls of the mixture into the prepared cake tin.

Bake in a moderately hot oven, gas mark 6, 400° F., for 25-30 minutes.

Remove from oven and leave for a few minutes before turning out onto cooling tray.

For variations, experiment with colours and flavours.

Substitute peppermint essence and green food colouring for pink; or use strong coffee and a little extra flour in place of the cocoa.

MOCK DANISH PASTRIES

Preparation Time: 15 minutes · Cooking Time: 10-15 minutes

7 oz. packet frozen but thawed puff pastry	2 level teaspoons ground cinnamon
2 oz. butter	Dried fruit
2 oz. caster sugar	Water icing

Roll the thawed pastry out to an oblong about 16 by 6 inches.

Cream the butter with the sugar and cinnamon and spread over the pastry.

Scatter dried fruit—chopped sultanas, dates, mixed peel, cherries, etc.—over it.

Roll up from the short end to make a fat roll.

Cut into ¾-inch slices and place on a baking sheet.

Bake in a hot oven, gas mark 8, 450° F., for 10-15 minutes until golden-brown and crisp.

When cold, decorate with water icing.

NUT AND CHOCOLATE SQUARES

Preparation Time: 15 minutes · Cooking Time: 30-35 minutes

8 oz. digestive biscuits	1 teaspoon vanilla essence
4 oz. chocolate dots	Large can sweetened condensed milk
3 oz. chopped walnuts	¼ teaspoon salt

Crush the biscuits or turn to crumbs using a blender.

Another way to do this is to place the biscuits in a plastic bag and crush with a rolling pin.

Place the chocolate dots in a bowl over a pan of hot water and stir until melted.

Combine all ingredients in a mixing bowl and stir until well-combined.

Line an 8-inch square baking tin with greaseproof paper and grease base and sides of tin. Turn the mixture into the tin.

Bake in a moderate oven, gas mark 4, 350° F., for 30-35 minutes until firm in the tin, then turn onto a cooling rack.

When cold, cut into 2-inch squares.

RAISIN OAT COOKIES

Preparation Time: 15 minutes · Cooking Time: 15-20 minutes

3½ oz. butter	1 teaspoon baking powder
6 oz. soft brown sugar	1 teaspoon vanilla
1 egg	6 oz. rolled oats
4 oz. plain flour	4 oz. raisins
½ teaspoon salt	

Place the butter and sugar in a saucepan and stir over a gentle heat until butter has melted and sugar dissolved.

Remove from heat, add unbeaten egg and beat until well blended.

Sift together the flour, salt and baking powder and stir into butter mixture. Add the vanilla, oats and raisins.

Place teaspoonful on greased baking sheets.

Bake in a moderate oven, gas mark 4, 350° F., for 15-20 minutes.

Cool on a wire rack.

STREUSEL COFFEE CAKE

Preparation Time: 15 minutes · Cooking Time: 30-35 minutes

6½ oz. sachet sponge mix	1 oz. plain flour
2 eggs	2 tablespoons fresh white
1 teaspoon coffee and chicory	breadcrumbs
essence	½ teaspoon cinnamon
1 tablespoon sugar	½ oz. butter

Make up the sponge mix using the eggs and adding the essence, but otherwise following directions on pack.

Combine the sugar, sifted flour, breadcrumbs and cinnamon in a basin. Rub in the butter.

Grease a 7-inch cake tin and place a round of greaseproof paper in the base. Turn the cake mix into the tin and sprinkle the spice mixture over the top.

Bake in a moderate oven, gas mark 5, 375° F., for 30-35 minutes or until cake is done when tested with a skewer.

Turn onto wire rack to cool.

20 minutes

DOUGHNUTS

Preparation Time: 20 minutes · Cooking Time: NIL

½ lb. self-raising flour
½ teaspoon mixed spice
½ teaspoon salt
2 oz. golden syrup
1 egg, beaten

1 oz. butter
2½ fl. oz. milk
Oil for deep frying
Caster sugar for coating

Sift dry ingredients into a bowl. Rub in butter.

Combine syrup, egg and milk and pour into flour. Mix quickly to a soft dough and roll out on a floured board to ¼-inch thickness.

Using a plain 2½-inch cutter, cut into rounds. Stamp out centres with a plain 1½-inch cutter.

Heat the oil and fry the doughnuts until golden on both sides.

Drain on absorbent paper: dredge with sugar while still hot.

NO-BEAT DUNDEE CAKE

Preparation Time: 20 minutes · Cooking Time: 3 hours 5 min.

2 oz. glacé cherries
½ pint water
10 oz. butter or margarine
8 oz. currants
8 oz. sultanas
4 oz. chopped mixed peel

Large can sweetened condensed milk
10 oz. plain flour
¾ teaspoon bicarbonate of soda
Pinch of salt
Split blanched almonds

Line and grease an 8-inch cake tin. Chop cherries.

Place cherries, water, butter or margarine, prepared fruit and milk in a saucepan. Bring to the boil; reduce heat and simmer gently for 3 minutes. Remove from heat and leave to cool.

Combine the flour, bicarbonate of soda and the salt, and sift onto the fruit mixture. Beat well and pour into the prepared tin. Arrange the almonds on top.

Bake in a moderately cool oven, gas mark 3, 325° F., for 3 hours.

Cool in tin for 5 minutes before turning out onto a wire rack to complete cooling.

The ingredients for this cake may be halved. In this case, bake in a 6-inch tin for 2 hours.

25 minutes

LEMON CURD

Preparation Time: 25 minutes · Cooking Time: NIL

4 lemons	4 oz. butter
1 lb. sugar	4 eggs, beaten

Grate lemon rind finely and place with sugar, butter and the juice of the lemons in a double boiler or in a bowl over hot water.

Stir with a wooden spoon over a moderate heat until sugar is dissolved and butter is melted.

Stir in the beaten eggs.

Continue to stir until mixture is thick enough to coat the back of the spoon.

Pour into warm jars. Cover.

Drinks

Drinks

Drinks - 5 minutes

CHOCOLATE COLA

Preparation Time: 5 minutes · Cooking Time: NIL

2 brickettes vanilla ice-cream
2 tablespoons chocolate milk-
shake powder

1 standard bottle or can of cola
drink

Cut the ice-cream into cubes.
Put the chocolate powder, cola and half the ice-cream into a
mixing bowl and whisk together for 2-3 minutes.
Pour into two glasses and top with the remaining ice-cream
cubes.
Sprinkle with a little extra chocolate powder.
Serve with straws and long spoons.
Serves 2.

COFFEE SHAKE

Preparation Time: 5 minutes · Cooking Time: NIL

2 tablespoons instant coffee
1 tablespoon sugar
1 tablespoon hot water

1 large can evaporated milk
1 brickette vanilla ice-cream

Dissolve the instant coffee and sugar in the hot water in a large
bowl.
Make the evaporated milk up to 1½ pints with cold water.
Add the milk and ice-cream to the coffee and whisk until frothy.
Serve immediately in tall glasses with straws.

GOLDEN ANGEL

Preparation Time: 5 minutes · Cooking Time: NIL

25 fl. oz. bottle pure apple juice
10 oz. bottle dry ginger

Lemon or orange rind
Glacé cherries

Combine the chilled apple juice and dry ginger in a jug.
Pour into cocktail glasses, adding a twist of lemon or orange
rind to each glass and 2 glacé cherries on a cocktail stick.
Serves 12.

LEMONADE

Preparation Time: 5 minutes · Cooking Time: NIL

4 lemons   2 pints water
4 tablespoons sugar

Cut very thin slices of peel (no pith) from the lemons.
Boil with sugar and water for 1 minute, stirring.
Cool.
Meanwhile, squeeze and strain the juice from the lemons.
Strain sweetened lemon water over juice.
Chill.
Serve with ice.

PEANUT BUTTER MILK SHAKE

Preparation Time: 5 minutes · Cooking Time: NIL

1 tablespoon peanut butter   ¾ cup milk
A scoop of ice-cream

Mix all ingredients together, preferably in a blender, but whisking will do.
Serve at once.

WARMING PUNCH

Preparation Time: 5 minutes · Cooking Time: NIL

2 bottles red wine   Little grated nutmeg
2 pints water   Sherry glass of cherry brandy
2 oz. honey

Heat all ingredients together and serve hot.

10 minutes

GINGERED RUM PUNCH

Preparation Time: 10 minutes · Cooking Time: NIL

Juice of 4 oranges	2 fl. oz. rum
1 teaspoon powdered ginger	4 cinnamon sticks
4 dessertspoons clear honey	

Heat ¾ pint water with the orange juice in a saucepan until almost boiling.

Place the ginger and honey in a heat-proof jug and add the rum.

Pour the hot orange juice into the jug and stir well.

Transfer punch to 4 heat-proof glasses and add a cinnamon stick to each glass.

Serve very hot.

15 minutes

GLÜHWEIN

Preparation Time: 15 minutes · Cooking Time: NIL

Cinnamon stick	6 cloves
½ pint water	Pinch ground nutmeg
3 strips lemon peel	Pinch mixed spice
2 oz. sugar	Bottle red wine

Crush the cinnamon stick slightly and place in a small pan with the remaining ingredients except the wine.

Bring to simmering point slowly, and simmer for 10 minutes.

Strain into a large saucepan and pour in the wine.

Reheat and serve immediately in warmed glasses. Do not allow the wine to boil.

Makes 12 glasses of wine.

20 minutes

CHRISTMAS EVE WARMER

Preparation Time: 20 minutes · Cooking Time: NIL

2 oranges	6 cinnamon sticks
2 lemons	½ bottle rum
6 cloves	¾ pint diluted lemon squash
1 teaspoon grated nutmeg	1 pint fresh weak tea

Peel the zest from the oranges and lemons and place in a saucepan with ½ pint boiling water. Add the cloves, nutmeg and 2 crushed cinnamon sticks. Simmer gently for 10 minutes. Strain.

Meanwhile, using a sharp knife, remove pith and outer skin from the fruit. Cut oranges and lemons into slices.

Return the strained spice mixture to the rinsed out saucepan together with the rum, lemon squash and fruit slices. Reheat to just under boiling point.

Make the tea, strain into the punch and add sugar to taste.

Stir until sugar has dissolved.

Serve in tall glasses with the remaining cinnamon sticks as stirrers.

Index